It's another Quality Book from CGP

This book has been carefully written for 10-11 year olds.

It contains lots of questions covering all the Maths in the Year 6 Programme of Study — all perfectly matched to the new National Curriculum making it ideal for the SATS in May 2016 and beyond.

There are also practice tests at the start and end of the book to make sure you really know your stuff.

What CGP is all about

Our sole aim here at CGP is to produce the highest quality books — carefully written, immaculately presented and dangerously close to being funny.

Then we work our socks off to get them out to you — at the cheapest possible prices.

Contents

Published by CGP

Editors:
Katherine Craig, Rob Harrison, Sarah Pattison, Camilla Simson, Ben Train.

Contributors:
Sue Foord, Simon Greaves, Alyson Smith.

ISBN: 978 1 84762 214 3

With thanks to Karen Wells and Mary-Ann Parsons for the proofreading.
Also thanks to Jan Greenway for the copyright research.

Thumb illustration used throughout the book © iStockphoto.com.

Contains public sector information licensed under the Open Government Licence v2.0.
http://www.nationalarchives.gov.uk/doc/open-government-licence/

Printed by Elanders Ltd, Newcastle upon Tyne.
Clipart from Corel®

Based on the classic CGP style created by Richard Parsons.

Text, design, layout and original illustrations © Coordination Group Publications Ltd. (CGP) 2014
All rights reserved.

About This Book

This Book is Full of Year 6 Maths Questions

You'll learn a lot of <u>new maths</u> in Year 6. This book has questions on <u>all the maths</u> for Year 6. It <u>matches</u> our <u>Year 6 Study Book</u>. This can help you if you get stuck.

This book covers the <u>Attainment Targets</u> for <u>Year 6</u> of the <u>2015 National Curriculum</u>. The topics covered are roughly equivalent to the <u>old Levels 4-6</u>.

The questions in Sections 1-8 are all <u>colour-coded</u> to show how <u>difficult</u> they are.

①   ②   ③

Easy   Harder   Challenge

The <u>answers</u> to all of the questions are at the <u>back of this book</u>.

This book also has <u>two Objectives Tests</u>.

The one at the <u>front of the book</u> is to test that you <u>remember</u> the maths you learnt in <u>Year 5</u>. The test at the <u>back of the book</u> is to see how well you know the maths in <u>this book</u>.

There are Learning Objectives on All Pages

Learning objectives say <u>what you should be able to do</u>. Use the <u>tick circles</u> to show how <u>confident</u> you feel.

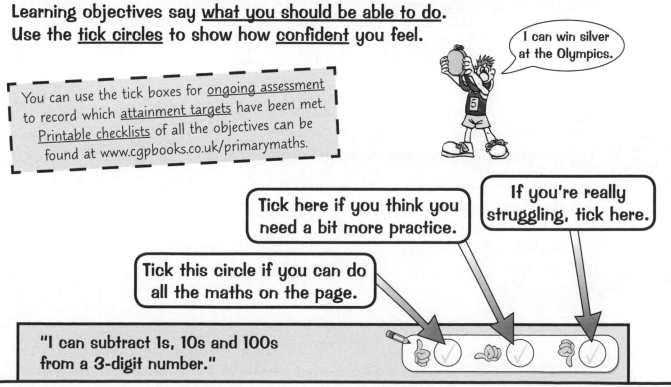

I can win silver at the Olympics.

You can use the tick boxes for <u>ongoing assessment</u> to record which <u>attainment targets</u> have been met. <u>Printable checklists</u> of all the objectives can be found at www.cgpbooks.co.uk/primarymaths.

Tick here if you think you need a bit more practice.

If you're really struggling, tick here.

Tick this circle if you can do all the maths on the page.

"I can subtract 1s, 10s and 100s from a 3-digit number."

Year Five Objectives Test

1 Shade 6 more squares on the grid below to make the pattern symmetrical in both mirror lines.

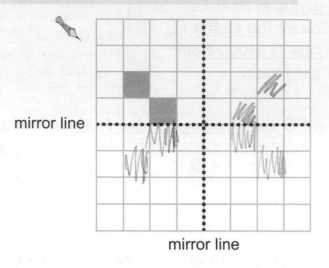

mirror line

mirror line

2 Here is an incomplete table showing the number of boys and girls in a school year who chose to study either French or German.

Complete the table.

	Boys	Girls	Total
French	20	25	45
German	30	15	45
Total	50	40	90

2 marks

3 Using a protractor, accurately measure the obtuse angle in this shape.

1 mark

4 Write these numbers in descending order.

~~476 040~~   ~~419 438~~   69 362   ~~413 870~~   ~~634 691~~

| 634,~~69~~ | 476,040 | 419,438 | 413,870 | 69,362 |

1 mark

5 Here is part of a net for a triangular prism.
Using a ruler, draw the missing face to complete the net.

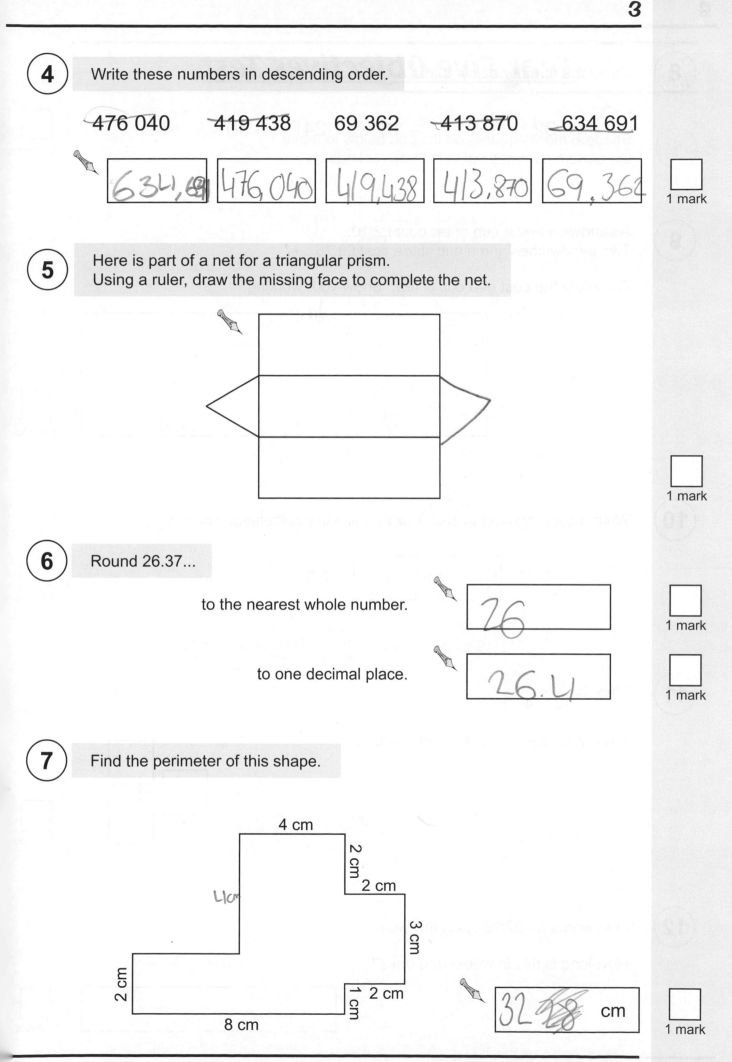

1 mark

6 Round 26.37...

to the nearest whole number.

26

1 mark

to one decimal place.

26.4

1 mark

7 Find the perimeter of this shape.

4 cm
2 cm
2 cm
4cm
3 cm
2 cm
1 cm
2 cm
8 cm

32 ~~28~~ cm

1 mark

8 Circle the number below that is a common multiple of 3 and 4.

32   21   18   (24)   30   44

1 mark

9 A sandwich and a cup of tea cost £2.10.
Two sandwiches and a cup of tea cost £3.70.

Calculate the cost of a cup of tea. Show your working.

50p   1 Sandwich = £1.60
           2.10
          -1.60
           0.50

2 marks

10 Write a cube number in each box to make this calculation correct.

64 + 1 = 65

1 mark

11 What is $\frac{7}{12} + \frac{3}{4}$?

$\frac{7}{12} + \frac{9}{12} =$

Write your answer as a mixed number.

$1 \frac{4}{12}$

$\times \frac{31}{7}$
$\frac{}{217}$

1 mark

12 Alan works for 225 days of the year.

How long is this in weeks and days?

32 weeks 1 day

1 mark

13 Carla has 4560 g of flour. She uses 1295 g to bake a cake.

How much flour does she have left?

$$\begin{array}{r} 4\,5\,6\,0 \\ -\;1\,2\,9\,5 \\ \hline 3\,2\,6\,5 \end{array}$$

3265 g

1 mark

14 Tony's patio is in an L-shape.

Find its area.

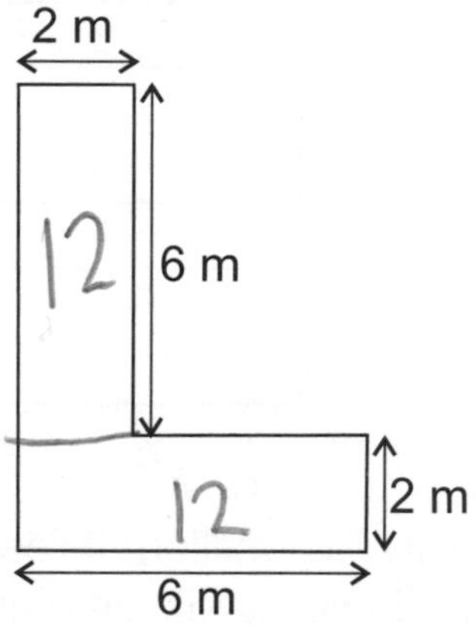

24 m²

2 m

12   6 m

12   2 m

6 m

1 mark

15 The diagram below shows three angles. It has not been drawn accurately.
Calculate the size of angle A.

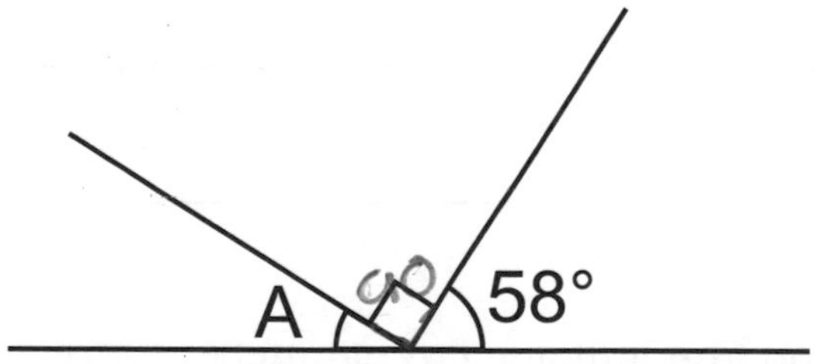

A   90   58°

32 °

1 mark

16 Jill and Riley each have a pizza.

Jill has eaten 45% of her pizza and Riley has eaten $\frac{3}{5}$ of his pizza.

Who has eaten the most pizza?

Riley

1 mark

17 Meryl is paid £1255 per month. How much does she earn in 25 months?

$$\begin{array}{r} 1255 \\ \times 25 \\ \hline 6125 \\ 24500 \\ \hline 30625 \end{array}$$

$$\begin{array}{r} 1255 \\ \times 25 \\ \hline 6125 \\ 24500 \\ \hline 30625 \end{array}$$

£ 30,625

1 mark

Total

YEAR FIVE OBJECTIVES TEST

Place Value in Very Large Numbers

1 What is the value of the digit '6' in the following numbers? Write your answers in words.

167

6~~0~~ Tens

1 mark

3640

6 hundreds

1 mark

648 210

6 hundred thousand

1 mark

2 Write out 'seventy two million, three hundred and one thousand, four hundred and twenty six' as a number.

72,301,426

1 mark

Is this number bigger or smaller than 72 310 462?

~~Smaller~~ B/ Smaller

1 mark

3 Put the following numbers in order, going from smallest to biggest:

~~65 887 206~~ Smallest: 56,887,206

~~56 887 206~~ 65,877,260

~~65 878 206~~ 65,878,206

65 887 026 65,887,026

65 877 260 Biggest: 65,887,206

1 mark

"I can read, write, order and compare numbers up to ten million."

Rounding Whole Numbers

1 Jack is rounding 4380 to the nearest hundred.

What are the two possible answers that this number lies between?

4300 and 4400 ☐ 1 mark

What is 4380 rounded to the nearest hundred?

4400 ☐ 1 mark

2 Circle the numbers below that round to 70 000 when they are rounded to the nearest thousand.

(70 069)   70 609   72 084

69 489   (69 984)   (70 284) ☐ 1 mark

Which number rounds to 70 000 when rounded to the nearest hundred?

69,984
~~70,284~~ ☐ 1 mark

3 Since opening, a museum has had 15 472 988 visitors.

Round the number of visitors to the nearest thousand.

15,473,000 ☐ 1 mark

Round the number of visitors to the nearest ten thousand.

15,705,470,000 ☐ 1 mark

Round the number of visitors to the nearest ten million.

20,000,000 ☐ 1 mark

"I can round any whole number." 👍✓ 🤷✓ 🤦✓

Calculating with Negative Numbers

1 At 1 am the soil temperature in Lucy's garden was –6 °C.
It rose to 4 °C by 1 pm.

What was the difference in temperature? Use the number line to help you.

```
+----+----+----+----+----+----+----+----+----+----+----+
-7   -6   -5   -4   -3   -2   -1   0    1    2    3    4
```

°C

1 mark

2 Work out these calculations. Use the number line to help you.

```
+----+----+----+----+----+----+----+----+----+----+----+
-7   -6   -5   -4   -3   -2   -1   0    1    2    3    4
```

–5 + 7 =

–7 + 4 =

2 marks

–1 – 5 =

1 – 5 =

2 marks

3 The table shows the temperature in different cities.

City	Temperature (°C)
London	-2
Birmingham	-7
Liverpool	-8
Manchester	2
Cardiff	0
York	-3
Glasgow	-4

What is the difference
in temperature between
Glasgow and Birmingham?

°C

1 mark

The temperature in York increases by 11 °C.
What is the temperature in York now?

°C

1 mark

"I can calculate using negative numbers."

Solving Number Problems

1 A dolphin is 27 m below the sea surface.

It swims 19 m towards the surface. How far is it from the surface now?

| m | | 1 mark |

From this new depth the dolphin jumps to a height of 7 m above the water. How far does it jump?

| m | | 1 mark |

2 Jane has £631 in her bank account.
John has −£117 in his bank account.

Round the amount of money in Jane's bank account to the nearest hundred.

| £ | | 1 mark |

Round the amount of money in John's bank account to the nearest hundred.

| −£ | | 1 mark |

How much more money does John need to have the same amount as Jane?

| £ | | 1 mark |

3 Fill in the gaps in the sentences below.

72 638 rounded to the nearest [   ] is 72 600.

| | 1 mark |

888 rounded to the nearest [   ] is 1000.

| | 1 mark |

47 459 202 rounded to the nearest [   ] is 47 000 000.

| | 1 mark |

"I can solve number problems."

SECTION ONE — NUMBER AND PLACE VALUE

Written Multiplication

1 Calculate:

152 × 82

238 × 37

2 marks

2 Calculate:

4118 × 28

2461 × 67

2 marks

3 There are 5631 boxes of pens in a warehouse. Each box contains 92 pens. How many pens are there in total? Show your working.

1 mark

"I can multiply a four-digit number by a two-digit number."

Written Division

1   Calculate:

576 ÷ 16

1512 ÷ 12

2 marks

2   Work out these divisions. Write any remainder as a fraction.

1699 ÷ 11

8888 ÷ 16

4 marks

3   At a wedding there are 2058 guests. Each table can seat 15 people.

Calculate how many tables are needed so that everyone has a seat. Show your working.

2 marks

How many empty seats will there be?

1 mark

"I can divide a four-digit number by a two-digit number and know what to do with remainders."

Mental Maths

This page is on **mental** maths, so you need to do these calculations in your head.

1 Work out these calculations in your head:

4321 + 3030

[ ] 1 mark

8000 − 2460

[ ] 1 mark

1200 × 12

[ ] 1 mark

2 An asteroid and a planet are 383 000 km apart.
The asteroid then travels 99 500 km towards the planet.

How far does the asteroid have left to travel before
it reaches the planet? Work it out in your head.

[km] [ ] 1 mark

3 Julian is 58 years old. To work out his son's age,
halve Julian's age and subtract eleven.

How old is Julian's son? Work it out in your head.

[ ] 1 mark

To find the age of Julian's mother, subtract seventeen
from his age and times by two.
How old is she? Work it out in your head.

[ ] 1 mark

4 The top of Mount Everest is 8848 m above sea level.
A point in the Mariana Trench is 10 911 m below sea level.

What is the difference in height between
these two points? Work it out in your head.

[m] [ ] 1 mark

"I can solve number problems and do
calculations with large numbers in my head." ✓ ✓ ✓

Estimating and Checking

1 Ross has worked out that 21.29 × 38 = 809.02.

What calculation could you do to check that this answer is about right?

1 mark

2 Paula estimates the answer to 28.33 × 6 by rounding.

What might her estimate be?

1 mark

3 Estimate the answer to 27.7 ÷ 5 by working out what numbers it lies between.

27.7 ÷ 5 is somewhere between ☐ and ☐

1 mark

4 The distance between Broughton-in-Furness and Grizebeck is 2.89 miles. There are 5280 feet in a mile.

Estimate the distance between Broughton-in-Furness and Grizebeck in feet.

feet

1 mark

"I can estimate to check the answer of a calculation."

BODMAS

1 Work out:

12 ÷ 4 + 2

1 mark

8 × (3 – 1)

1 mark

5 × 3 – 5

1 mark

2 Insert brackets to make the calculations true:

6 + 6 × 3 – 3 = 33

1 mark

2 + 5 × 7 – 3 = 28

1 mark

3 Work out:

12 ÷ (4 – 2) × 3

1 mark

4 Georgia has four pizzas, each divided into nine slices. She wants to share the pizzas equally between herself and five friends.

Circle the number sentence that she could use to work out how many slices of pizza each person gets.

(4 × 9) ÷ (1 + 5)   (4 ÷ 9) × (1 + 5)   4 × 9 ÷ 1 + 5

1 mark

How many slices of pizza does Georgia get?

slices

1 mark

"I know what order to do things in a calculation."

Multiples, Factors and Primes

1 What is the lowest common multiple of 9 and 12?

1 mark

2 Give three common factors of 24 and 36.

1 mark

3 Circle all the prime numbers in the list below.

1   11   21   31   41   51   61   71   81   91

1 mark

4 Fill in the boxes with prime numbers to complete this calculation.

☐ × ☐ × ☐ = 66

1 mark

5 A game show host asks you to count up to 30. If you ring a bell when you say a multiple of three <u>or</u> five, you win £1. If you ring a bell exactly twice when you say a multiple of three <u>and</u> five, you win £5.

What is the maximum amount of money you can win?

£

2 marks

"I know how to find common multiples, common factors and prime numbers."

Solving Calculation Problems

1 I am thinking of a number. If I add 24 to it and then subtract 18 I get 36.

What number am I thinking of?

1 mark

2 In a school P.E. cupboard there are 5 sacks of netballs, 6 sacks of footballs and 4 sacks of basketballs. Each sack holds 10 balls.

How many balls are there altogether?

balls

1 mark

Mr Jenkins takes out 2 sacks of footballs and 1 sack of netballs for a lesson. How many balls are left in the P.E. cupboard?

balls

1 mark

3 Rachel has four bags of sweets. In each bag there are twelve sweets. She wants to share them equally between eight people.

How many sweets does each person get?

sweets

1 mark

4 Dan buys 6 tins of paint. Each tin contains 3 litres. He uses 4 litres of paint in the dining room and 5 litres of paint in the lounge.

How many tins of paint has he used?

tins

1 mark

He needs 6 litres of paint to decorate the hall. Does he have enough left?

1 mark

Solving Calculation Problems

5 Sam is 23. In seven years' time, he will be twice as old as his sister is now.

How old is Sam's sister now?

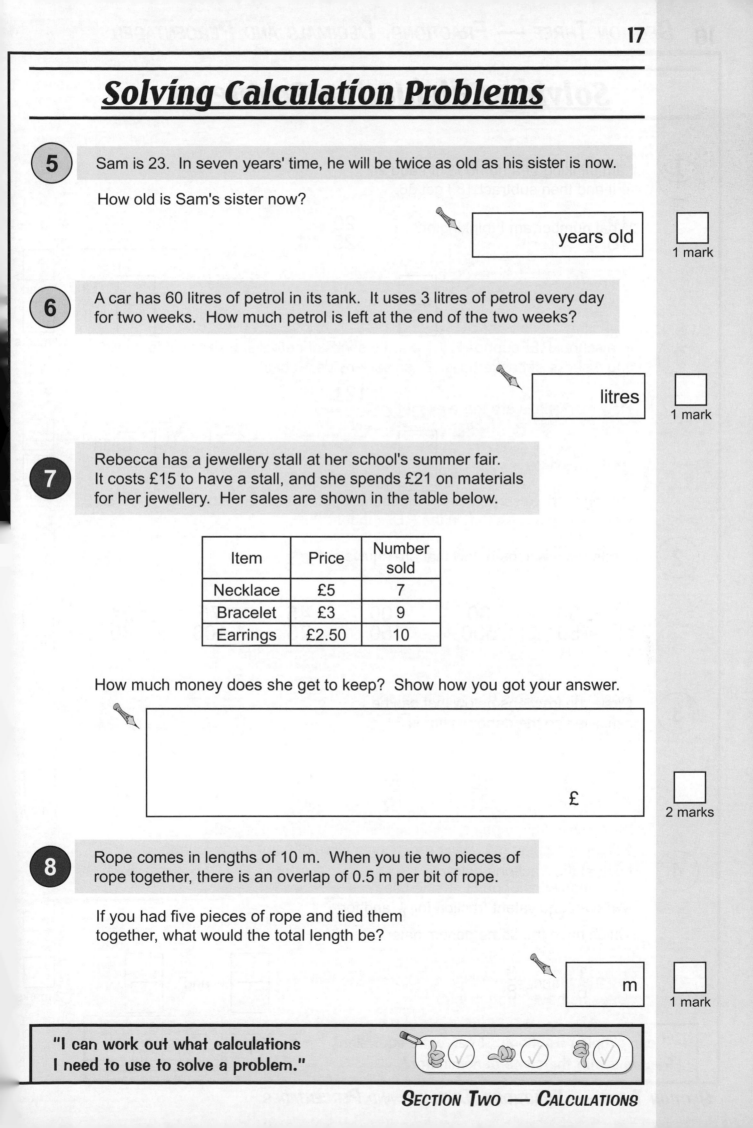

| | years old | | 1 mark |

6 A car has 60 litres of petrol in its tank. It uses 3 litres of petrol every day for two weeks. How much petrol is left at the end of the two weeks?

| | litres | | 1 mark |

7 Rebecca has a jewellery stall at her school's summer fair. It costs £15 to have a stall, and she spends £21 on materials for her jewellery. Her sales are shown in the table below.

Item	Price	Number sold
Necklace	£5	7
Bracelet	£3	9
Earrings	£2.50	10

How much money does she get to keep? Show how you got your answer.

| £ | | 2 marks |

8 Rope comes in lengths of 10 m. When you tie two pieces of rope together, there is an overlap of 0.5 m per bit of rope.

If you had five pieces of rope and tied them together, what would the total length be?

| | m | | 1 mark |

"I can work out what calculations I need to use to solve a problem."

Simplifying Fractions

1   Simplify these fractions.

$$\frac{12}{16}$$

$$\frac{20}{25}$$

$\boxed{}$

$\boxed{}$

2 marks

$$\frac{12}{72}$$

$$\frac{33}{121}$$

$\boxed{}$

$\boxed{}$

2 marks

2   Circle the fractions below that are equivalent to $\frac{3}{5}$.

$$\frac{30}{50} \qquad \frac{30}{500} \qquad \frac{100}{150} \qquad \frac{45}{75} \qquad \frac{75}{100} \qquad \frac{24}{40}$$

1 mark

3   Circle the fractions below that can be simplified so the denominator is 3.

$$\frac{9}{12} \qquad \frac{18}{21} \qquad \frac{5}{15} \qquad \frac{250}{300} \qquad \frac{27}{81} \qquad \frac{6}{12}$$

1 mark

4   Look at the fractions below.

Write an equivalent fraction for $\frac{1}{6}$ and for $\frac{3}{8}$ which have the same denominator.

$$\frac{1}{6} \quad \text{and} \quad \frac{3}{8}$$

$\boxed{}$ and $\boxed{}$

2 marks

"I can simplify fractions. I can write equivalent fractions with the same denominator."

<u>*Ordering Fractions*</u>

1 Put the fractions $\frac{1}{2}$, $\frac{3}{5}$ and $\frac{4}{20}$ in order from smallest to largest.

smallest   largest

1 mark

2 Put the fractions $\frac{2}{3}$, $\frac{4}{5}$ and $\frac{8}{15}$ in order from largest to smallest.

largest   smallest

1 mark

3 Put these improper fractions and mixed numbers in order from smallest to largest.

$1\frac{7}{8}$ $2\frac{1}{8}$

$\frac{12}{8}$ $\frac{14}{8}$

smallest   largest

1 mark

4 Put these improper fractions in order from smallest to largest.

$\frac{5}{3}$ $\frac{6}{5}$

$\frac{3}{2}$ $\frac{7}{6}$

smallest   largest

1 mark

"I can compare and order fractions, including fractions greater than 1."

Adding and Subtracting Fractions

1 Calculate:

$$\frac{1}{8} + \frac{1}{4}$$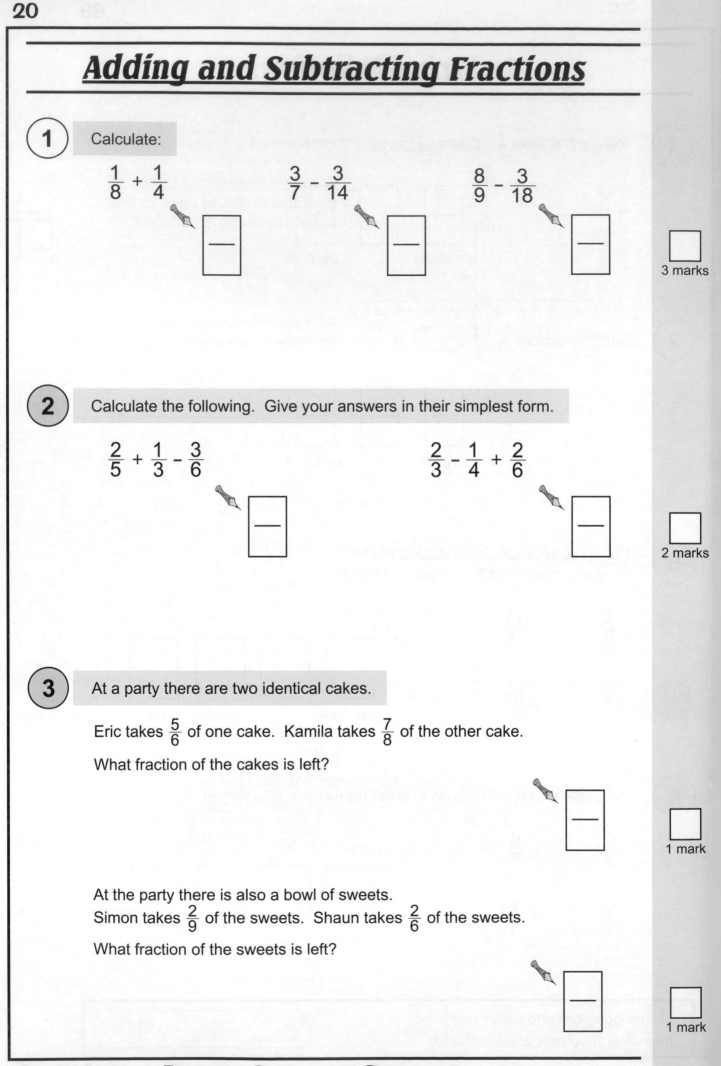

$$\frac{3}{7} - \frac{3}{14}$$

$$\frac{8}{9} - \frac{3}{18}$$

3 marks

2 Calculate the following. Give your answers in their simplest form.

$$\frac{2}{5} + \frac{1}{3} - \frac{3}{6}$$

$$\frac{2}{3} - \frac{1}{4} + \frac{2}{6}$$

2 marks

3 At a party there are two identical cakes.

Eric takes $\frac{5}{6}$ of one cake. Kamila takes $\frac{7}{8}$ of the other cake.

What fraction of the cakes is left?

1 mark

At the party there is also a bowl of sweets.
Simon takes $\frac{2}{9}$ of the sweets. Shaun takes $\frac{2}{6}$ of the sweets.

What fraction of the sweets is left?

1 mark

Adding and Subtracting Fractions

4 Calculate the following. Write your answers as mixed numbers.

$$4\frac{6}{11} + \frac{7}{22}$$

$$\frac{35}{12} - 1\frac{5}{8}$$

2 marks

5 Fill in the missing numbers below.

$$\frac{25}{4} + \frac{\boxed{}}{4} = 7\frac{6}{8}$$

$$2\frac{2}{11} - \frac{\boxed{}}{22} = \frac{14}{11}$$

2 marks

6 Which of the following calculations gives the largest fraction?
Circle the correct answer. Show your working.

$$\frac{18}{5} + \frac{4}{3} \qquad\qquad \frac{12}{10} - \frac{1}{3} \qquad\qquad 2\frac{1}{2} + \frac{7}{3}$$

2 marks

"I can add and subtract fractions
by using a common denominator."

Multiplying Fractions

1 Calculate:

$$\frac{1}{3} \times \frac{1}{5}$$

$$\frac{1}{4} \times \frac{1}{9}$$

2 marks

2 What is $\frac{1}{3} \times \frac{3}{4}$?

Write your answer in its simplest form.

1 mark

3 Which of the following calculations gives the largest fraction?
Circle the correct answer. Show your working.

$$\frac{1}{4} \times \frac{2}{5} \qquad \frac{3}{8} \times \frac{4}{5} \qquad \frac{3}{10} \times \frac{2}{3}$$

2 marks

"I can multiply fractions by other fractions."

Dividing Fractions by Whole Numbers

1 Calculate:

$\frac{1}{2} \div 5$

$\frac{1}{8} \div 3$

2 marks

$\frac{1}{4} \div 8$

$\frac{1}{12} \div 6$

2 marks

2 Calculate the following. Write your answers in their simplest form.

$\frac{6}{11} \div 3$

$\frac{14}{15} \div 4$

2 marks

3 Jesse has a bottle of lemonade. One third has already been drunk. He shares the rest between himself and three other friends.

What fraction of the full bottle do they each get?
Write your answer in its simplest form.

1 mark

"I can divide fractions by whole numbers."

Multiplying or Dividing by 10, 100 or 1000

1 What is the value of the digit '8' in the following numbers?

6.847

1 mark

289.355

1 mark

0.078

1 mark

2 Calculate:

211.2 ÷ 100   18 × 1000

2 marks

3 What do you need to divide the following numbers by so that the answer has three decimal places? Circle the correct answers.

98.8   10   100   1000

1 mark

101.01   10   100   1000

1 mark

32   10   100   1000

1 mark

"I can multiply or divide numbers by 10, 100 or 1000."

Multiplying with Decimals

1 Work out these multiplications.

0.6 × 8

0.09 × 7

2 marks

2 Work out these multiplications.

2.4 × 7

6.18 × 9

2 marks

3 A bus ticket to the beach costs £3.45.

Seven friends buy bus tickets to the beach. How much do they pay in total?

BUS TICKET £3.45

£

1 mark

A train ticket costs £4.10. If they each got a train ticket instead, how much more money would they pay in total?

£

1 mark

"I can multiply decimal numbers by whole numbers."

Dividing with Decimals

1 Work out the following divisions.

0.09 ÷ 3

0.12 ÷ 6

2 marks

2 Work out the following divisions.

10.08 ÷ 8

206.4 ÷ 6

2 marks

3 Hayley buys 9 plastic cups for a picnic. Each cup is the same price.

She pays £3.87 in total. What is the price of one cup?

£

1 mark

4 Leo has a plank of wood that is 128.8 cm long.

He cuts the plank into 8 equal pieces.
How long is each piece?

cm

1 mark

"I can divide decimal numbers
by whole numbers."

Rounding Decimals

1 Circle all the numbers below that come to 2.6 when you round to the nearest 0.1.

2.65   2.61   2.66   2.59   2.56   2.55   2.60

1 mark

2 Round these numbers to 1 decimal place.

11.23

0.09

3.456

2 marks

3 Round these numbers to 2 decimal places.

14.282

0.215

27.595

2 marks

4 Which of the numbers below could be rounded to the nearest tenth to give 13.0?

Circle the correct answers.

13.168   13.018   12.941   12.956

1 mark

5 Jon thinks of a number with 3 decimal places.
He rounds it down to 4.36. What was the original number?

Write down the 4 possibilities.

1 mark

"I can round decimal numbers
to a given number of decimal places."

SECTION THREE — FRACTIONS, DECIMALS AND PERCENTAGES

28

Fractions, Decimals and Percentages

1 Place these values in order from smallest to largest.

$$\frac{69}{100} \qquad 0.66 \qquad 67\% \qquad \frac{34}{50}$$

smallest   largest

1 mark

2 For each pair of values, circle the bigger amount.

0.65   or $\frac{3}{5}$

1 mark

73%   or $\frac{37}{50}$

1 mark

$\frac{3}{25}$ or   0.15

1 mark

0.38   or $\frac{9}{25}$

1 mark

3 Fill in the missing numbers below.

$0.44 = \dfrac{\Box}{25} = \Box \%$

2 marks

$0.8 = \dfrac{20}{\Box} = \Box \%$

2 marks

SECTION THREE — FRACTIONS, DECIMALS AND PERCENTAGES

Fractions, Decimals and Percentages

4 Miss Norfolk and Mr Jukes are marking books. They each have the same number of books to mark. Miss Norfolk has marked 75% of her books. Mr Jukes has marked $\frac{19}{25}$ of his books.

Who has marked the most books? Show your working.

1 mark

5 Circle the three equivalent amounts listed below.

$\frac{4}{40}$ 20%   0.02 $\frac{2}{20}$

40% $\frac{4}{20}$ 0.2 $\frac{2}{5}$

1 mark

6 Jim wins £1600 and gives 30% of it to charity.
Jack wins £1500 and gives $\frac{2}{5}$ of it to charity.

Who gives more money to charity? Show your working.

2 marks

7 Convert $\frac{5}{8}$ to a decimal.

1 mark

"I can convert fractions to decimals by dividing. I can convert between fractions, decimals and percentages."

Relative Sizes

1 A doughnut costs 35p. How much will 5 doughnuts cost?

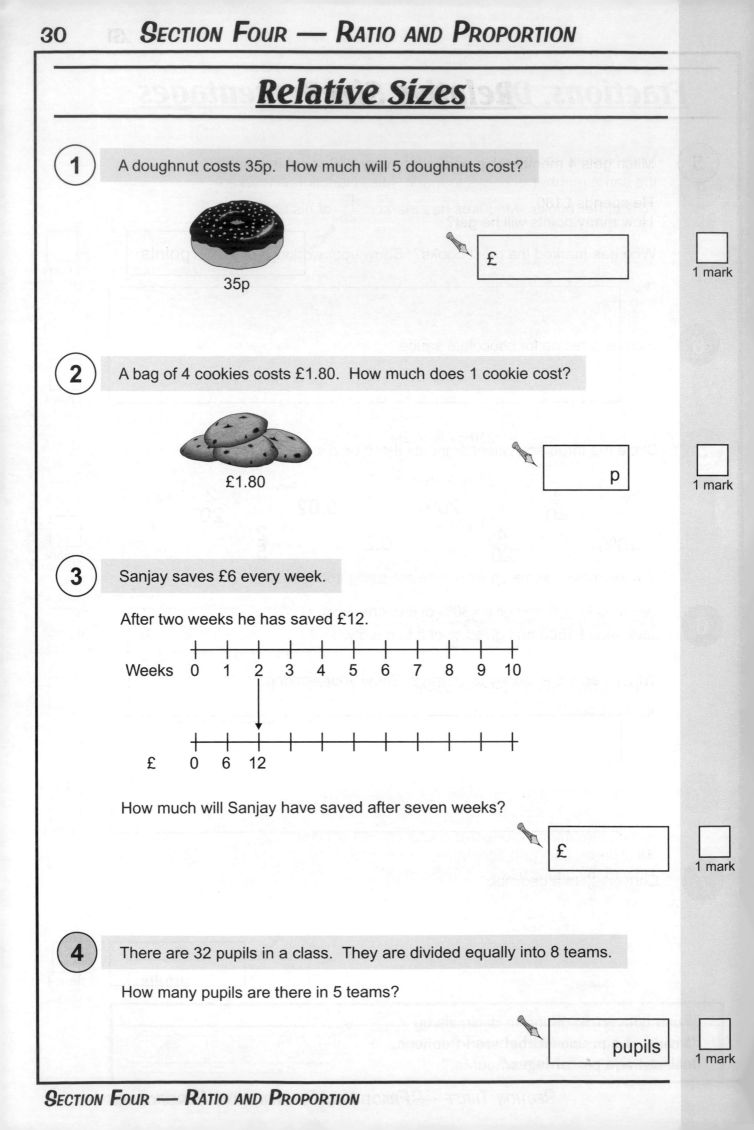

35p

£ ☐

1 mark

2 A bag of 4 cookies costs £1.80. How much does 1 cookie cost?

£1.80

☐ p

1 mark

3 Sanjay saves £6 every week.

After two weeks he has saved £12.

```
Weeks   0   1   2   3   4   5   6   7   8   9   10

   £    0   6  12
```

How much will Sanjay have saved after seven weeks?

£ ☐

1 mark

4 There are 32 pupils in a class. They are divided equally into 8 teams.

How many pupils are there in 5 teams?

☐ pupils

1 mark

Relative Sizes

5 Mitch gets 4 membership points for every £30 spent in a shop.

He spends £180.
How many points will he get?

points

1 mark

6 Here is a recipe for chocolate sauce.

> ### Recipe
>
> 250 g Chocolate
>
> 150 g Butter
>
> 75 g Sugar

James makes some chocolate sauce using 450 g butter.

How much chocolate does he need?

g

1 mark

What is the ratio of butter to sugar
in the recipe?

1 mark

7 A school holds a quiz to raise money for charity.

Each team must include two adults and six children.
48 children take part altogether.
How many adults take part in the quiz?

adults

1 mark

"I can solve problems that are to do with
the relative sizes of two amounts."

SECTION FOUR — RATIO AND PROPORTION

Scale Factors

1 Enlarge shape H by a scale factor of 2. Draw your answer on the grid below.

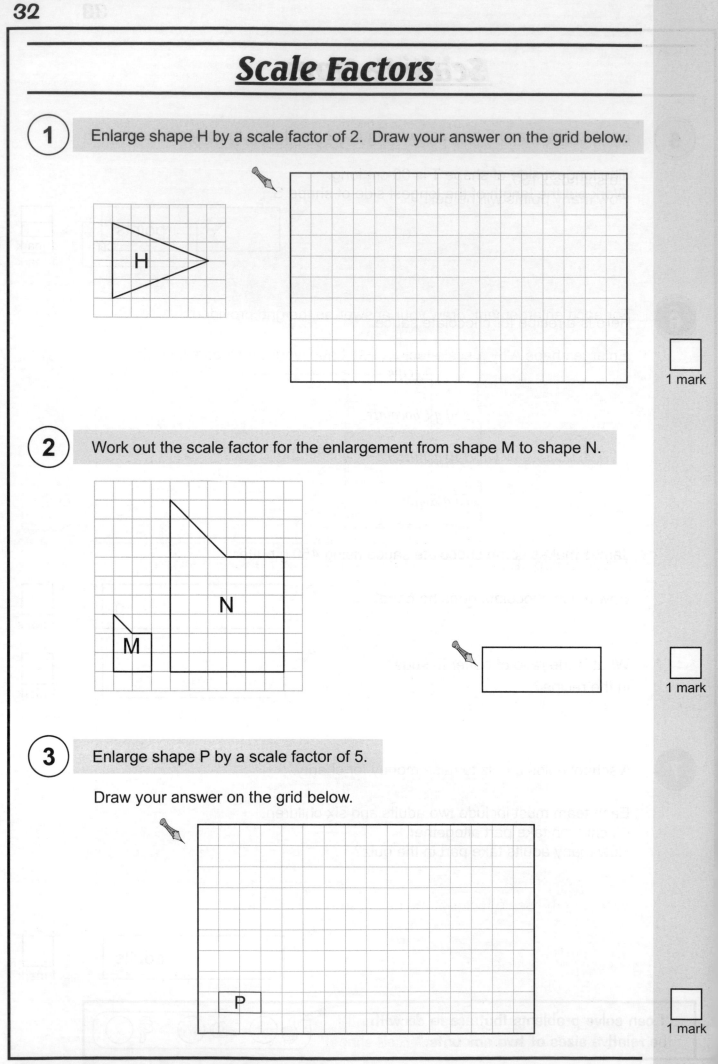

1 mark

2 Work out the scale factor for the enlargement from shape M to shape N.

1 mark

3 Enlarge shape P by a scale factor of 5.

Draw your answer on the grid below.

1 mark

Scale Factors

4 Ed enlarges shape S by a scale factor of 12, and labels the enlarged shape T.

The longest side of shape T is 60 cm long.
Work out the length of the longest side of shape S.

[ ] cm

1 mark

5 For each enlargement, draw your answer on the grid provided.

Enlarge shape A by a scale factor of 3. Label your enlarged shape B.

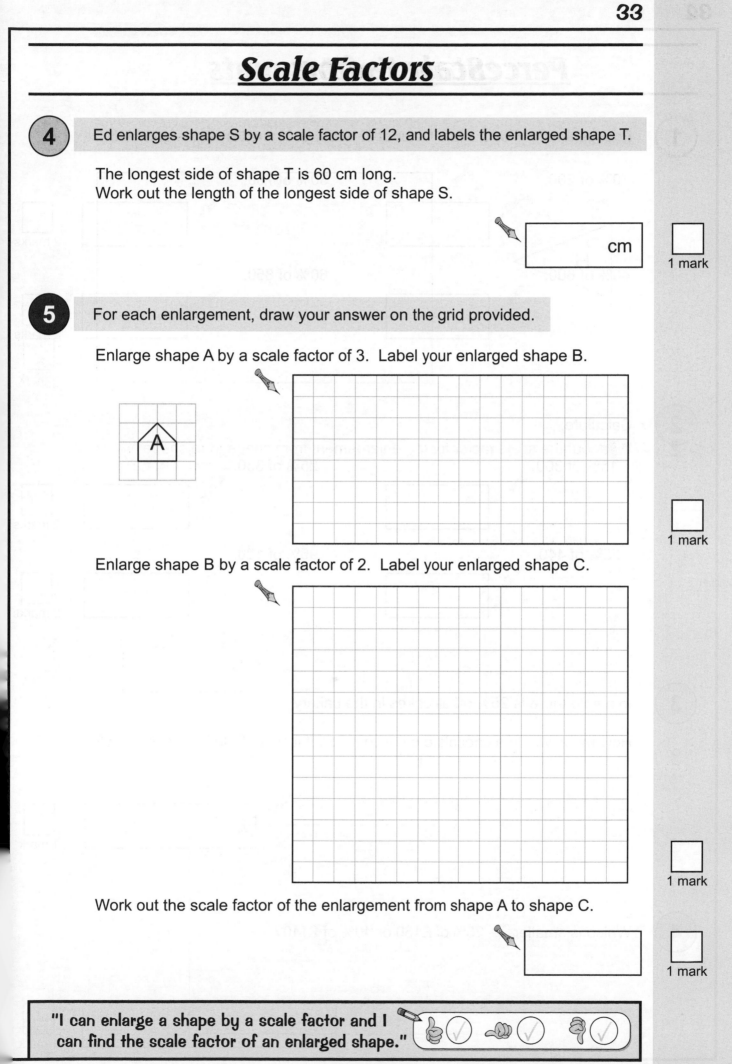

1 mark

Enlarge shape B by a scale factor of 2. Label your enlarged shape C.

1 mark

Work out the scale factor of the enlargement from shape A to shape C.

1 mark

"I can enlarge a shape by a scale factor and I can find the scale factor of an enlarged shape."

Percentages of Amounts

1 Calculate:

10% of 200.

30% of 750.

2 marks

40% of 600.

60% of 850.

2 marks

2 Calculate:

15% of 300.

25% of 360.

2 marks

55% of 440.

95% of 120.

2 marks

3 In a sale there is 25% off all cakes in the bakery.

How much would a chocolate cake cost now if it cost £3.80 before the sale?

£

1 mark

4 Which is smaller — 25% of £160 or 40% of £140?

1 mark

Percentages of Amounts

5 There are 360° in a circle. Paula eats 65% of a circular cake.

How many degrees of the cake has she eaten?

| °|

1 mark

6 In a survey of 120 people, 45% said that they prefer crisps to biscuits at lunch time.

How many people prefer biscuits at lunch time?

1 mark

7 In a clothing sale, jumpers are 20% off and t-shirts are 15% off.
Jumpers cost £12 before the sale and t-shirts cost £8 before the sale.

Dan buys 2 jumpers and a t-shirt in the sale.
How much does he spend?

£

1 mark

How much does he save off the original price?

£

1 mark

"I can find a percentage of an amount."

Comparing Using Percentages

1 Harry needs £400 to buy a new computer. He has saved £160 so far.

What percentage has Harry saved?

$$\frac{160}{400} \quad \frac{40}{100}$$

[____] %

1 mark

2 Farmer Fred has 200 sheep on his farm.

He sells 40 of them.
What percentage of his sheep does he have left?

$$\frac{40}{200} \quad \frac{1}{5} \quad \frac{200}{}$$

[____] %

1 mark

3 The price of a car is reduced from £1500 to £1050.

By what percentage is the price reduced?

$$\frac{1500}{1050} \qquad \frac{450}{1500} \quad \frac{90}{300} \quad \frac{30 \; 3}{10}$$

[____] %

1 mark

4 Abu has a bag of coloured balls.
The bag contains 5 red balls, 8 blue balls and 7 yellow balls.

What percentage of the balls are blue?

[____] %

1 mark

Comparing Using Percentages

5 Kayleigh and Rachael each buy clothes in a sale.

Kayleigh's clothes normally cost £50 but had £5 off.
Rachael's clothes normally cost £20 but had £3 off.

Whose clothes had the biggest percentage discount?

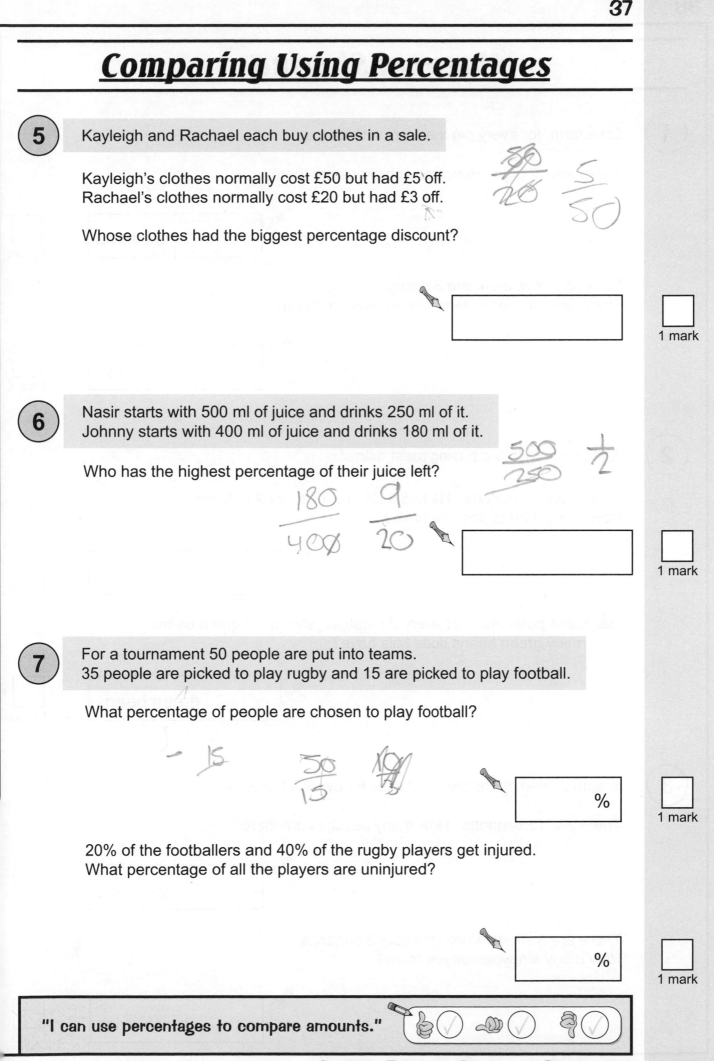

1 mark

6 Nasir starts with 500 ml of juice and drinks 250 ml of it.
Johnny starts with 400 ml of juice and drinks 180 ml of it.

Who has the highest percentage of their juice left?

1 mark

7 For a tournament 50 people are put into teams.
35 people are picked to play rugby and 15 are picked to play football.

What percentage of people are chosen to play football?

%

1 mark

20% of the footballers and 40% of the rugby players get injured.
What percentage of all the players are uninjured?

%

1 mark

"I can use percentages to compare amounts."

Unequal Sharing

1 On a farm, for every pig there are 4 chickens.

There are 12 pigs. How many chickens are there?

chickens

1 mark

For every cow, there are 3 sheep.
There are 15 sheep. How many cows are there?

cows

1 mark

2 James and Mila are having roast dinner.

James has 6 potatoes. He has 3 carrots for every 2 potatoes.
How many carrots does he have?

carrots

1 mark

Mila has 4 potatoes. For every 2 potatoes, she has 7 green beans.
How many green beans does Mila have?

green beans

1 mark

3 In a fruit salad, there are 4 peaches for every 6 bananas.

There are 18 bananas. How many peaches are there?

peaches

1 mark

There are 5 strawberries for every 3 bananas.
How many strawberries are there?

strawberries

1 mark

Unequal Sharing

4 At the zoo, the reptile house contains only snakes and lizards.
For every 3 snakes there are 2 lizards.

There are 100 animals in the reptile house.
How many lizards are there?

| lizards |

1 mark

5 In a football match, for every 2 goals that
Georgetown score, Hatville score 5 times.

14 goals are scored in total.
How many goals did each team score?

Georgetown [ ]   Hatville [ ]

2 marks

6 Ben and Keera share 8 cheese sandwiches and 9 ham sandwiches.

Ben takes 3 cheese sandwiches for every 1 of Keera's.
Keera takes 2 ham sandwiches for every 1 of Ben's.

How many sandwiches does Ben get in total?

| sandwiches |

1 mark

"I can work out how to share things unequally."

Sequences

1 A number sequence goes 1, 13, 25, 37, 49.

What is the rule to get from one term to the next?

☐ 1 mark

2 The rule for the sequence below is "add 5".

Write down the next three terms in the sequence.

6   11

☐ 1 mark

3 The rule for the sequence below is "subtract 4".

Write down the next three terms in the sequence.

36   32

☐ 1 mark

4 Write the next two terms in the sequence.

29   22   15

☐ 1 mark

5 Fill in the missing numbers in the sequence.

-12   -6   6   12

☐ 1 mark

Sequences

6 Write the first two terms in the sequence.

☐   ☐   87   98   109   ☐ 1 mark

7 A number sequence goes 37, 30, 23, 16, 9.

What is the rule to get from one term to the next?

☐ 1 mark

What is the 8th term in the sequence?

☐ 1 mark

8 The rule for the sequences below is "subtract the same number each time".

Find the two numbers missing from the sequence.

7   ☐   ☐   –5   ☐ 1 mark

Find the three numbers missing from the sequence.

53   ☐   ☐   ☐   9   ☐ 1 mark

"I can generate and describe number sequences." 👍✓ 🤚✓ 👎✓

Missing Number Problems

1 John and Sam are brothers. Sam is 3 years old. John is j years old.

If you multiply John's age by 3 and subtract 12, you get Sam's age:

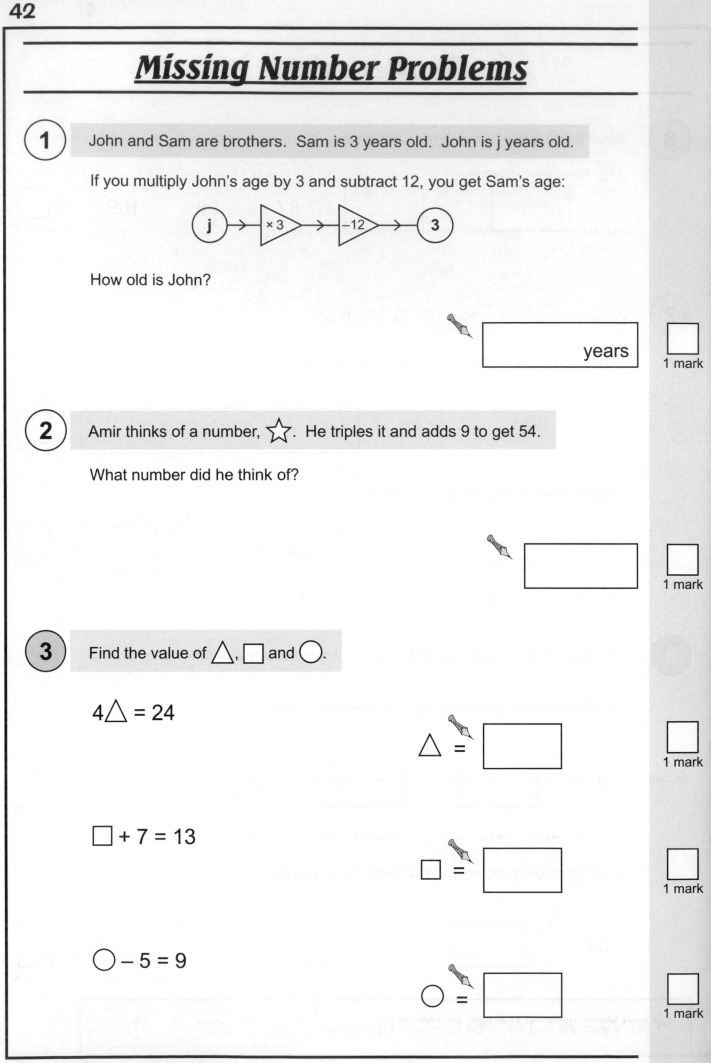

How old is John?

years

1 mark

2 Amir thinks of a number, ☆. He triples it and adds 9 to get 54.

What number did he think of?

1 mark

3 Find the value of △, ☐ and ◯.

$4 \triangle = 24$

△ =

1 mark

$\square + 7 = 13$

☐ =

1 mark

$\bigcirc - 5 = 9$

◯ =

1 mark

Missing Number Problems

4 Pierre and Jen collect badges. Pierre has 3 times as many badges as Jen.

This can be shown by p = 3j, where p = the number of badges Pierre owns and j = the number of badges Jen owns.

If Pierre has 12 badges, how many does Jen have?

	badges

1 mark

5 Matt has m muffins. Rob has r muffins.
Rob has twice as many muffins as Matt.

Which of the following shows this? Circle the correct answer.

2m = r   m = 2r   5m = 10r

1 mark

6 A caterpillar eats c leaves and a slug eats s leaves.
The caterpillar eats 4 times more leaves than the slug.

Which of the following shows this? Circle the correct answer.

4s = 8c   2c = 4s   c = 4s

1 mark

7 In a strawberry and banana smoothie the number of bananas is one sixth the number of strawberries, minus one.

Emma's smoothie contains 2 bananas and s strawberries.
How many strawberries are in Emma's smoothie?

	strawberries

1 mark

"I can solve missing number problems using symbols and letters."

Two Missing Numbers

1 Given that A × B = 12, list 3 different pairs of values for A and B.

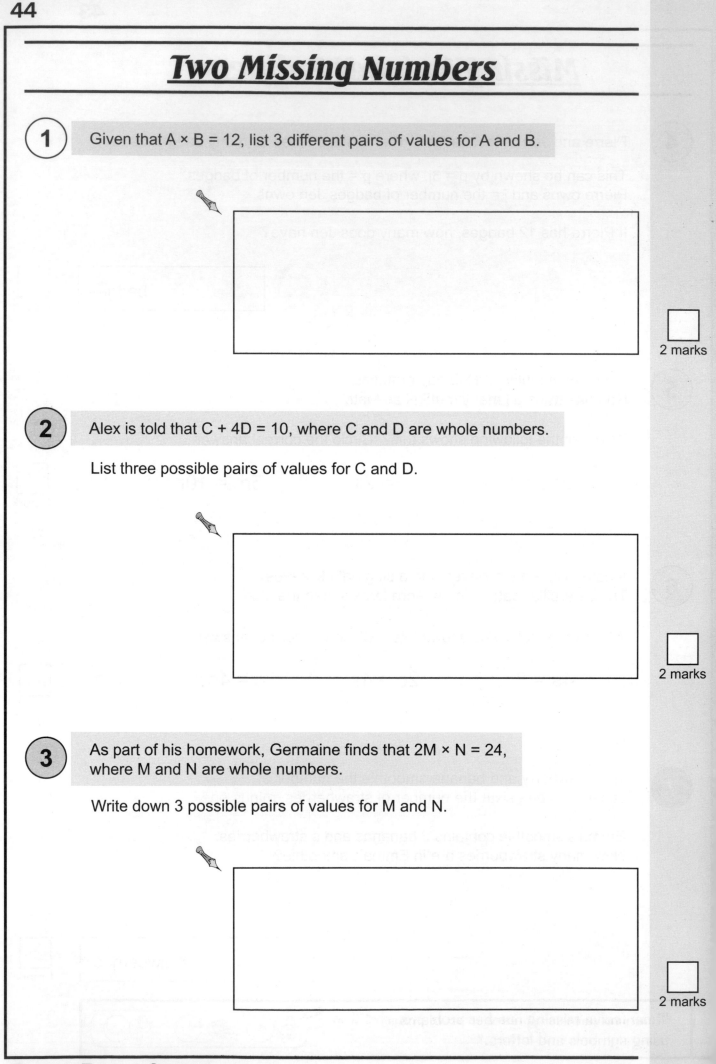

2 marks

2 Alex is told that C + 4D = 10, where C and D are whole numbers.

List three possible pairs of values for C and D.

2 marks

3 As part of his homework, Germaine finds that 2M × N = 24, where M and N are whole numbers.

Write down 3 possible pairs of values for M and N.

2 marks

Two Missing Numbers

4 Raj spends exactly £6 on ice creams and sandwiches.
Ice creams are £1 and sandwiches are £2.

To show this Raj writes down: i + 2s = 6,
where i = ice creams and s = sandwiches.

List all the possible pairs of values for i and s.

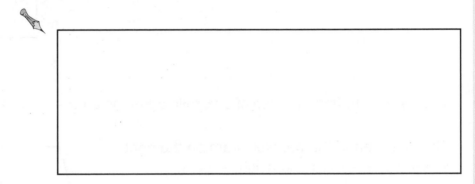

2 marks

5 Here are 5 number cards. I, J and K stand for different whole numbers.

The sum of all the cards is 36.
If I = 10, write down 3 possible pairs of values for J and K.

2 marks

"I can find pairs of numbers to solve problems with two unknowns, and list all possible combinations."

Formulas

1 Dillan is having a party. He wants to buy some cookies for his guests.

The number of cookies in a bag is given by the formula:
number of cookies = 8 × number of bags.

If Dillan buys 4 bags, how many cookies will he have?

	cookies

2 The formula to find the area of a parallelogram is area = base × height.

Find the area of the parallelogram on the right,
where base = 7 cm and height = 4 cm.

4 cm

7 cm

Not to scale.

	cm²

3 The amount of flour (in grams) needed to make
any number of cupcakes is given by this formula:
amount of flour = 11 × number of cupcakes + 10.

How much flour is needed to make 12 cupcakes?

	g

4 The formula for the time needed in minutes to cook a turkey is:

$$\text{Time} = \frac{160 \times \text{weight (kg)} + 80}{4}$$

How long does it take to cook a turkey that weighs 4 kg?

	minutes

Formulas

5 In a game, a team scores 5 points per goal.

Write a formula in words for the number of points that they score per goal.

Points = [   ]

1 mark

6 In a shop, apples cost 16p each.

Write a formula in words for the total cost (in pence)
of buying any number of apples.

Cost = [   ]

1 mark

Calculate how much 3 apples will cost.

Cost = [p]

1 mark

7 At a country fair, it costs 5p to play the hoopla, plus 2p per hoop.

Write a formula in words for the total cost (in pence)
of playing the hoopla with any number of hoops.

Cost = [   ]

1 mark

What is the total cost of playing the hoopla with 8 hoops?

Cost = [p]

1 mark

"I can use formulas written in words."

Units

1   Rita fills a bucket with 10.8 litres of water.

How much is this in ml?

ml

1 mark

2   Sadaf buys 258 g of oranges.

How much is this in kg?

kg

1 mark

3   One portion of pasta has a mass of 60 g.

How many portions are there in a 1.2 kg bag of pasta?

portions

1 mark

4   Olive oil costs £3.50 for 1 litre.

How much would 200 ml of olive oil cost?

£

1 mark

5   It takes Sam 1 year, 4 weeks and 5 days to cycle around the world.

How many days is this?

days

1 mark

Units

6 Gareth drives his car for 24 km. Approximately how many miles is this?

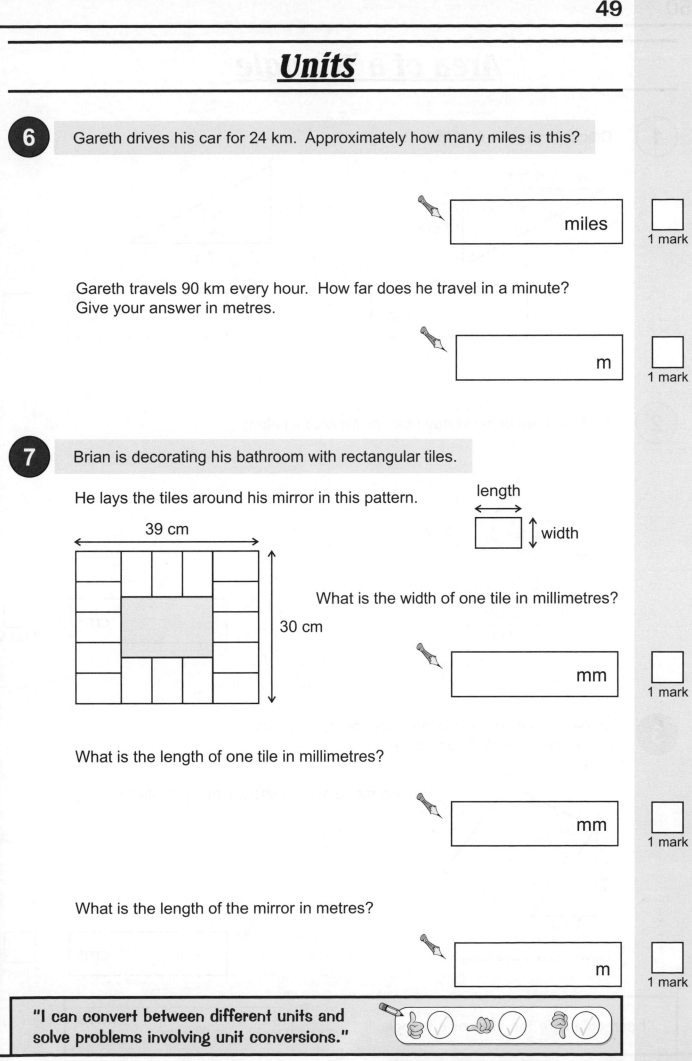

[ ] miles

1 mark

Gareth travels 90 km every hour. How far does he travel in a minute?
Give your answer in metres.

[ ] m

1 mark

7 Brian is decorating his bathroom with rectangular tiles.

He lays the tiles around his mirror in this pattern.

39 cm

30 cm

length

width

What is the width of one tile in millimetres?

[ ] mm

1 mark

What is the length of one tile in millimetres?

[ ] mm

1 mark

What is the length of the mirror in metres?

[ ] m

1 mark

"I can convert between different units and solve problems involving unit conversions."

SECTION SIX — MEASUREMENT

Area of a Triangle

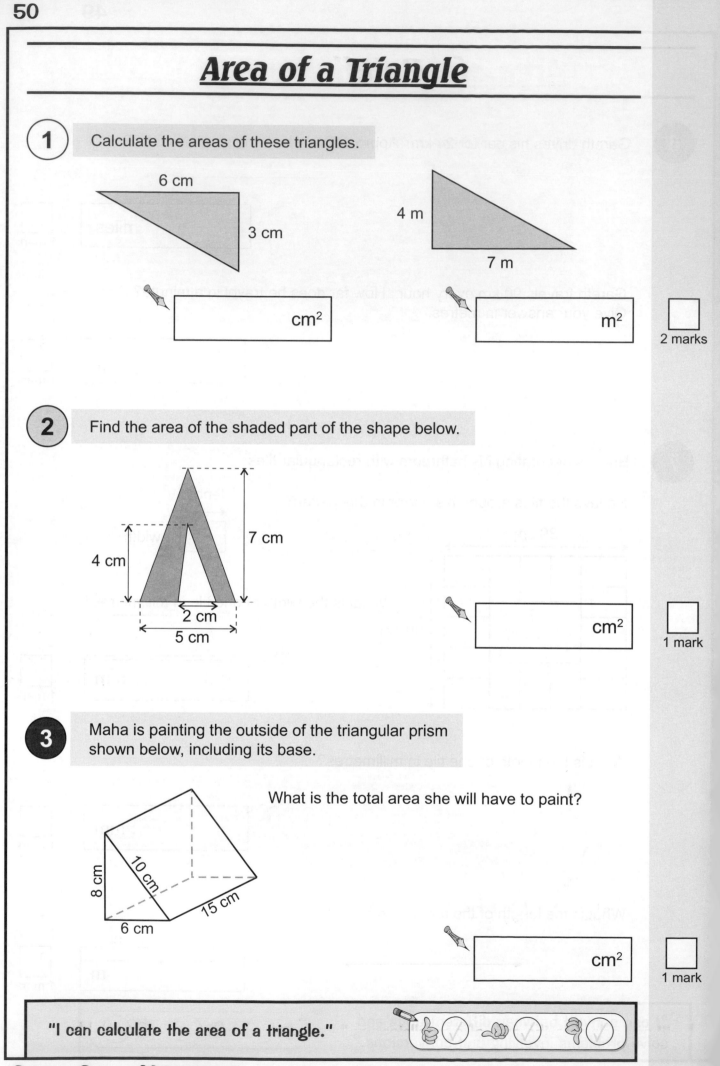

1 Calculate the areas of these triangles.

6 cm

3 cm

4 m

7 m

cm²

m²

2 marks

2 Find the area of the shaded part of the shape below.

7 cm

4 cm

2 cm

5 cm

cm²

1 mark

3 Maha is painting the outside of the triangular prism shown below, including its base.

What is the total area she will have to paint?

8 cm

10 cm

15 cm

6 cm

cm²

1 mark

"I can calculate the area of a triangle."

Area of a Parallelogram

1 Calculate the areas of these parallelograms.

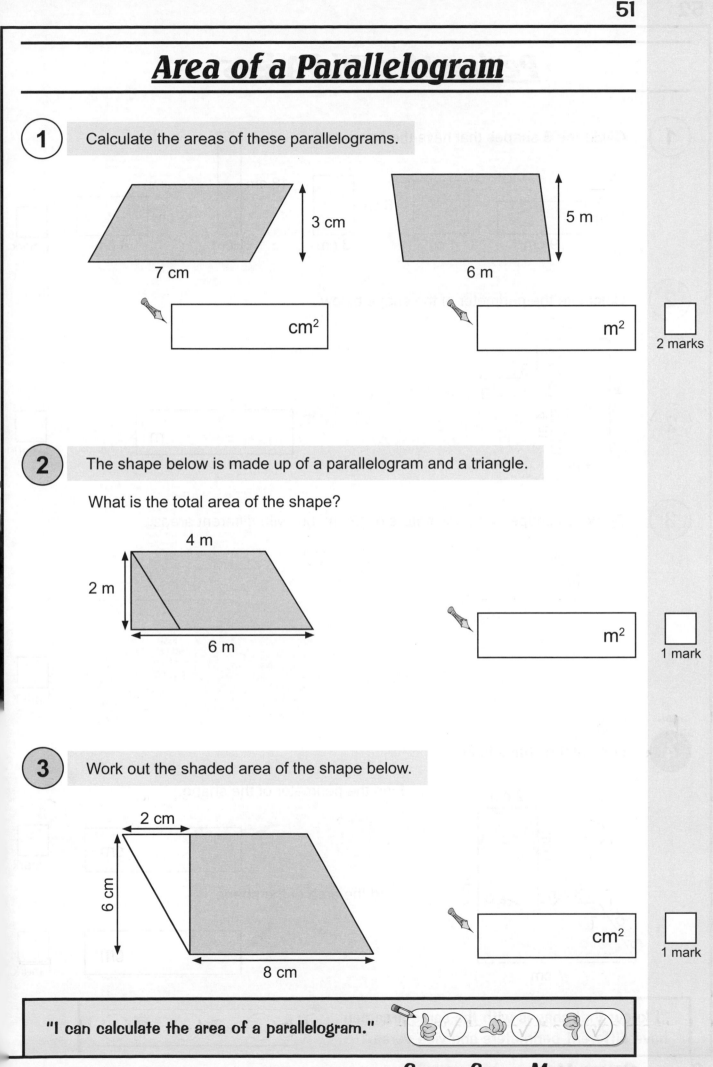

3 cm

7 cm

[   ] cm²

5 m

6 m

[   ] m²

2 marks

2 The shape below is made up of a parallelogram and a triangle.

What is the total area of the shape?

4 m

2 m

6 m

[   ] m²

1 mark

3 Work out the shaded area of the shape below.

2 cm

6 cm

8 cm

[   ] cm²

1 mark

"I can calculate the area of a parallelogram."

<u>Perimeters and Areas</u>

1 Circle the 3 shapes that have the same area.

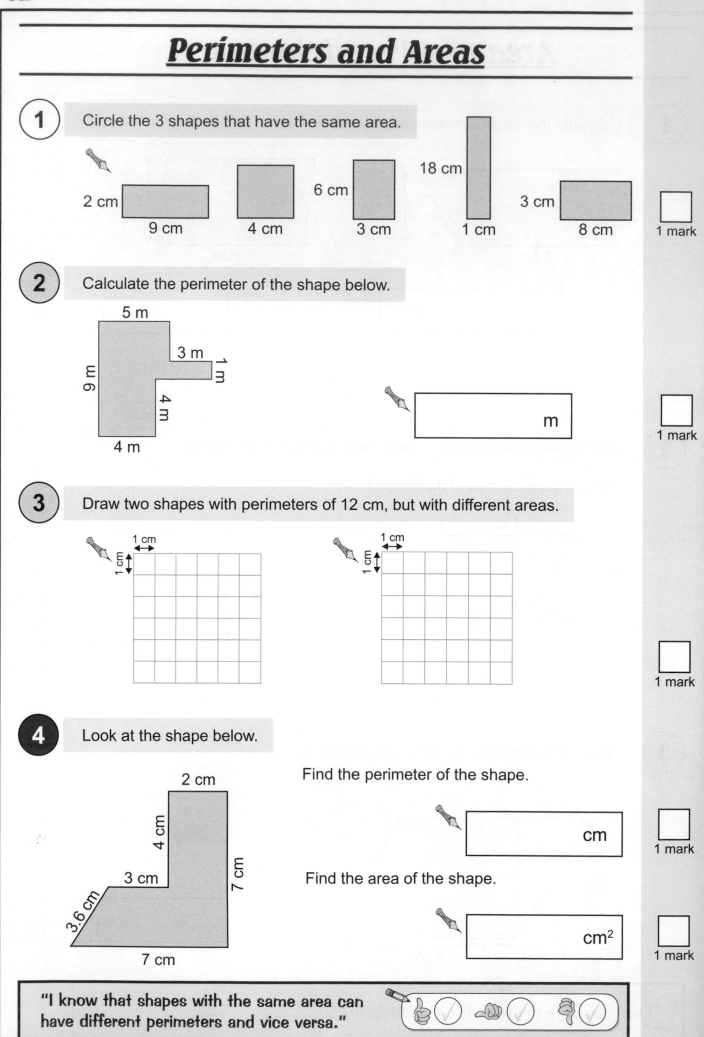

2 cm
9 cm

4 cm

6 cm
3 cm

18 cm
1 cm

3 cm
8 cm

1 mark

2 Calculate the perimeter of the shape below.

5 m
3 m
1 m
9 m
4 m
4 m

m

1 mark

3 Draw two shapes with perimeters of 12 cm, but with different areas.

1 cm
1 cm

1 cm
1 cm

1 mark

4 Look at the shape below.

2 cm
4 cm
3 cm
7 cm
3.6 cm
7 cm

Find the perimeter of the shape.

cm

1 mark

Find the area of the shape.

cm²

1 mark

"I know that shapes with the same area can have different perimeters and vice versa."

Volumes of Cubes and Cuboids

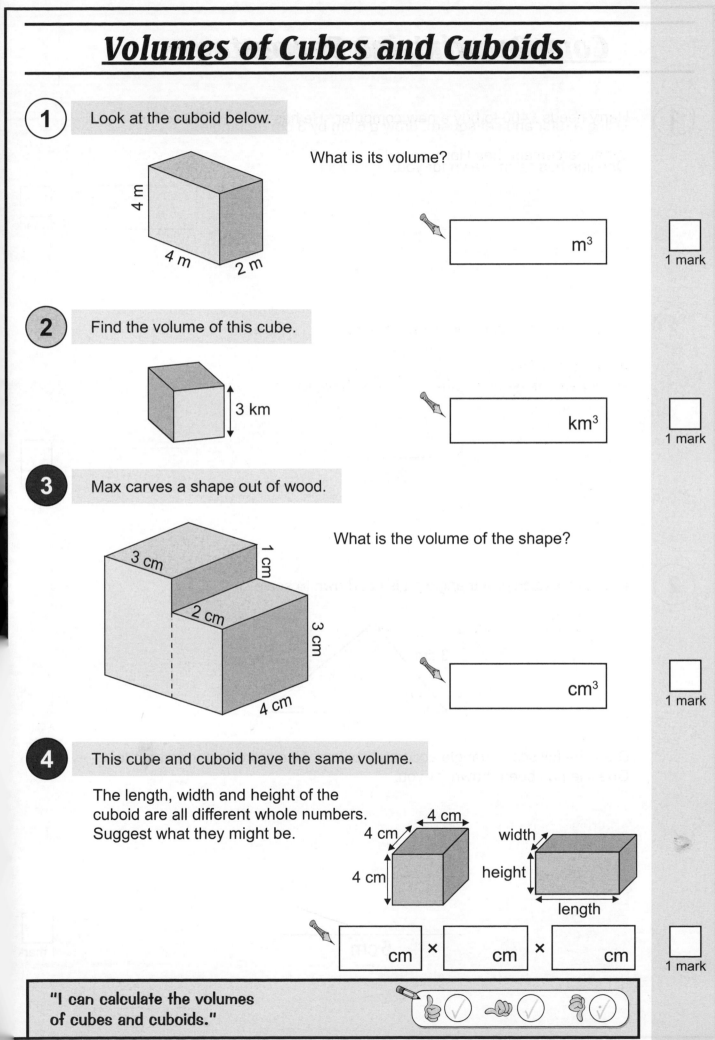

1 Look at the cuboid below.

4 m
4 m   2 m

What is its volume?

[m³]

1 mark

2 Find the volume of this cube.

3 km

[km³]

1 mark

3 Max carves a shape out of wood.

3 cm
1 cm
2 cm
3 cm
4 cm

What is the volume of the shape?

[cm³]

1 mark

4 This cube and cuboid have the same volume.

The length, width and height of the
cuboid are all different whole numbers.
Suggest what they might be.

4 cm
4 cm
4 cm

width
height
length

[cm] × [cm] × [cm]

1 mark

"I can calculate the volumes
of cubes and cuboids."   ✓   ✓   ✓

Drawing 2D Shapes

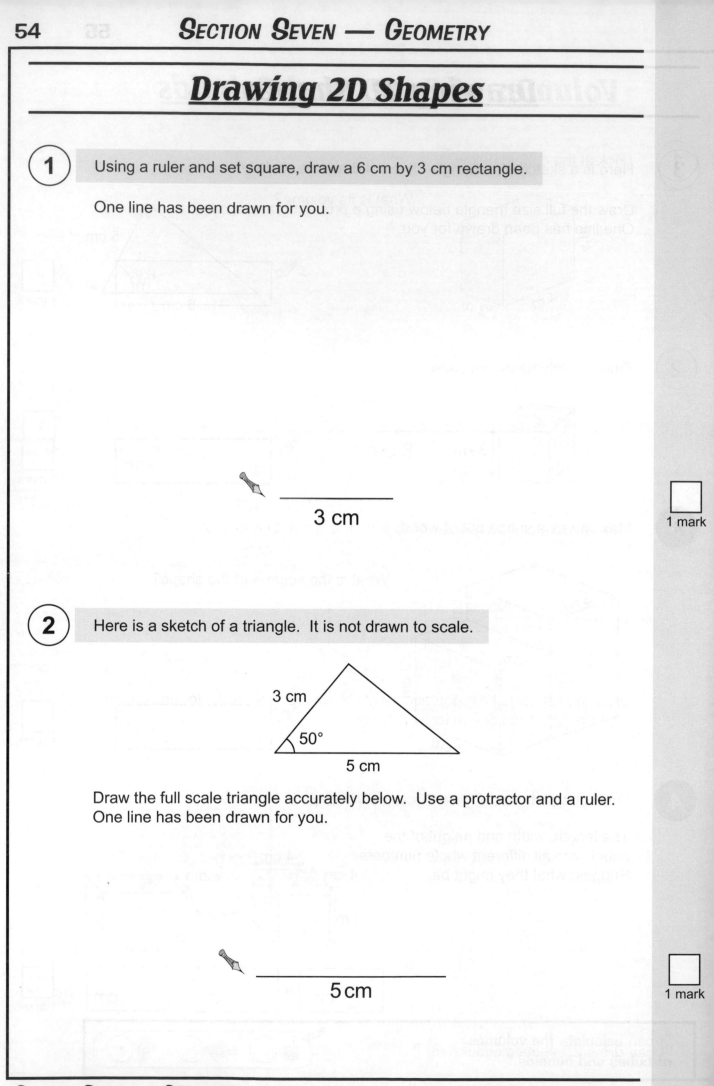

(1) Using a ruler and set square, draw a 6 cm by 3 cm rectangle.

One line has been drawn for you.

3 cm

(2) Here is a sketch of a triangle. It is not drawn to scale.

3 cm

50°

5 cm

Draw the full scale triangle accurately below. Use a protractor and a ruler.
One line has been drawn for you.

5 cm

Drawing 2D Shapes

3 Here is a sketch of a triangle. It is not drawn to scale.

Draw the full size triangle below using a protractor and a ruler.
One line has been drawn for you.

5 cm

63°

8 cm

8 cm

4 Here is a sketch of a regular hexagon. It is not drawn to scale.

3 cm

120°

Draw the full scale hexagon accurately below. Use a protractor and a ruler.
One line has been drawn for you.

3 cm

"I can draw 2D shapes accurately."

Making 3D Shapes

1 Look at this cuboid.

Circle all the shapes needed to make up its net.

1 mark

2 Circle the 3D shapes below that have one or more triangles as part of their nets.

tetrahedron

cone

cylinder

cube

square-based pyramid

1 mark

3 The diagram below shows the same cube from 4 different angles.

Draw symbols in the correct places to complete the net for this cube.

Net:

1 mark

"I can recognise, describe and build 3D shapes. I can make nets."

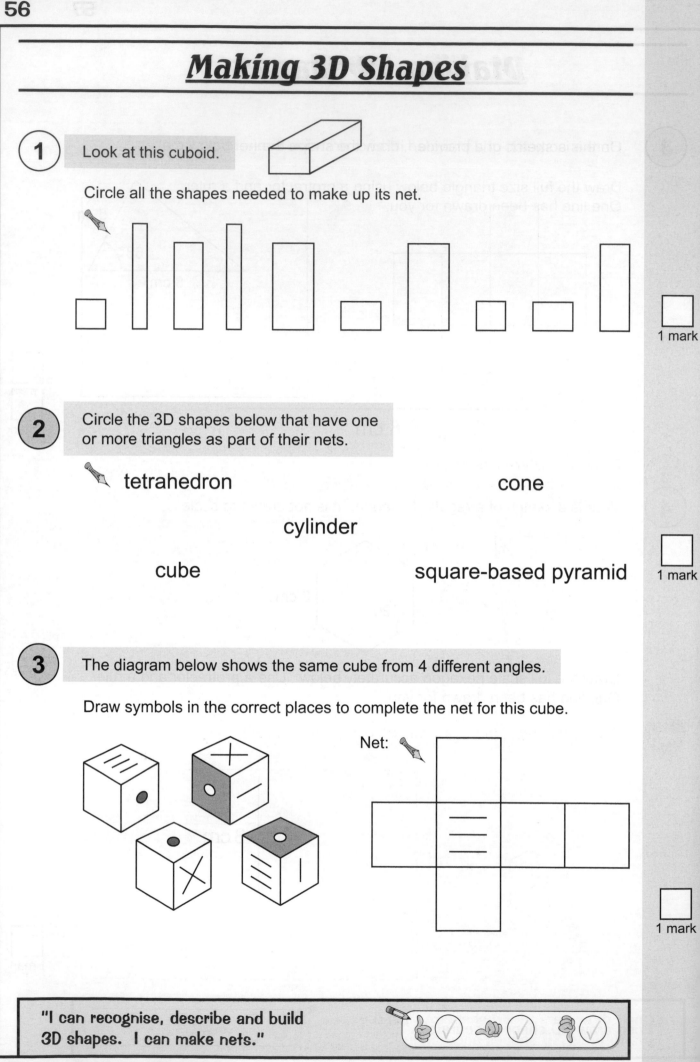

Making 3D Shapes

4 On the isometric grid provided, draw the shape the net below makes.

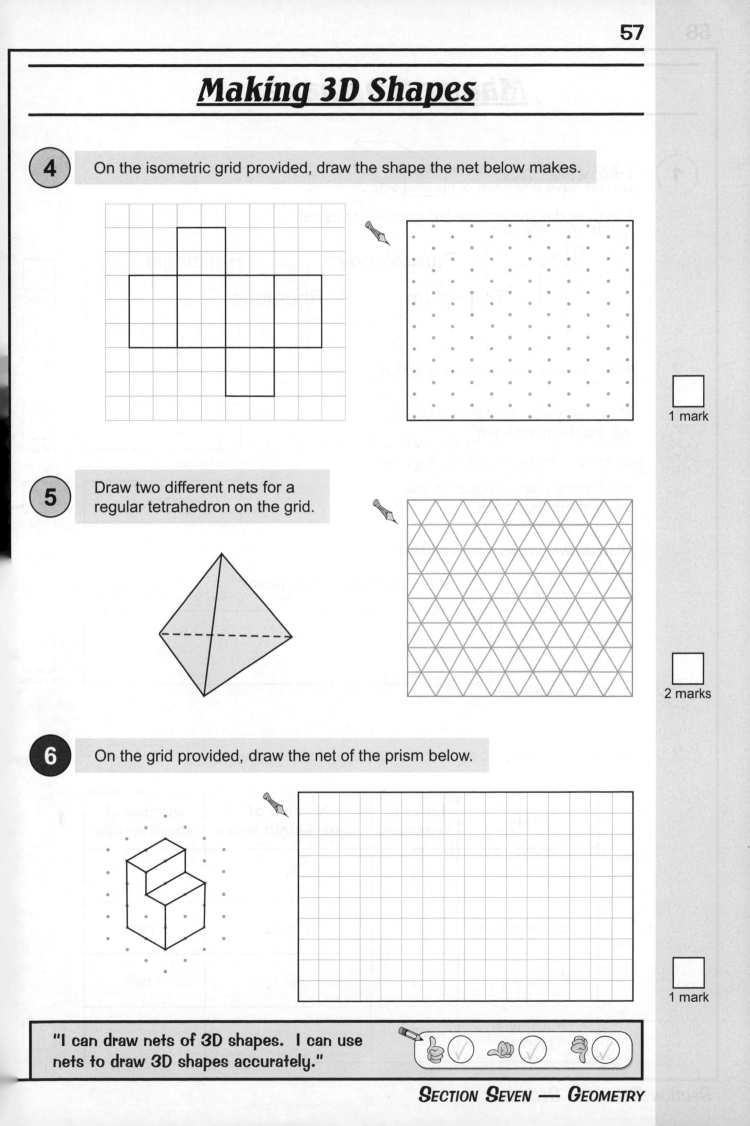

1 mark

5 Draw two different nets for a regular tetrahedron on the grid.

2 marks

6 On the grid provided, draw the net of the prism below.

1 mark

"I can draw nets of 3D shapes. I can use nets to draw 3D shapes accurately."

Shape Properties

1 Which two of the quadrilaterals below do **not** have two pairs of parallel sides?

Circle your answers.

Kite   Parallelogram   Rectangle

Trapezium   Rhombus

1 mark

2 Vlad draws a rhombus and a square.

How many equal-length sides
will his rhombus have?

1 mark

How many pairs of equal angles
will his rhombus have?

1 mark

Vlad draws arrows on his square
like this:

What do these arrows mean?

1 mark

3 Complete the table to show the properties of some polygons.

Shape	Lines of symmetry	Number of equal-length sides	Number of equal angles
	8	8	8
parallelogram		2 pairs	2 pairs
kite	1		1 pair
equilateral triangle	3	3	

2 marks

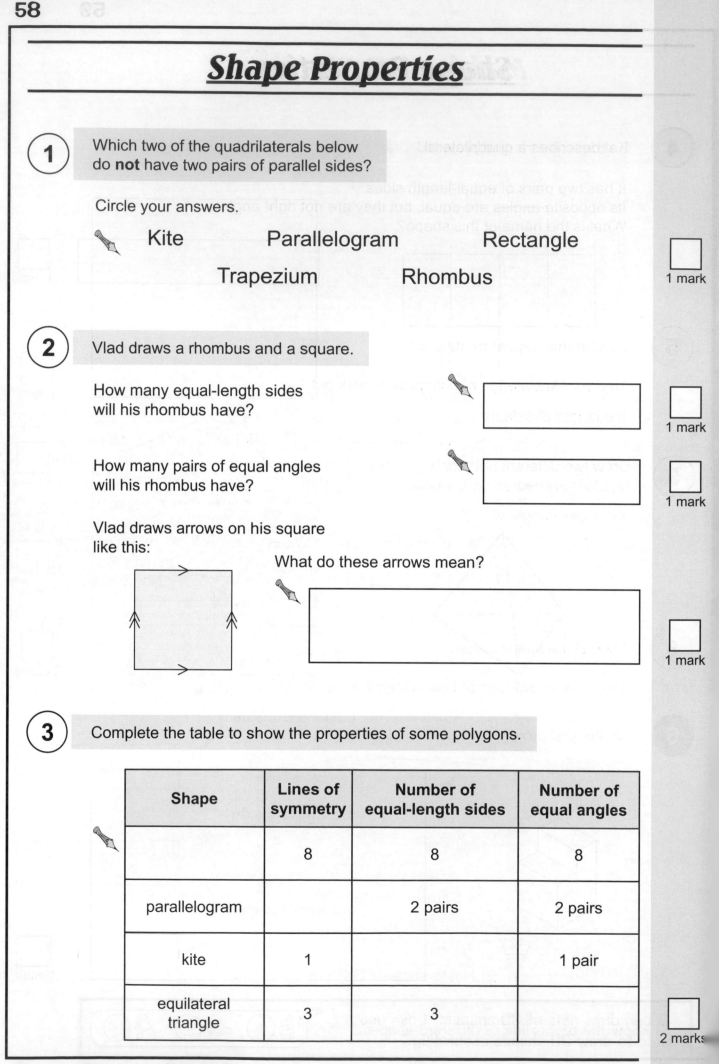

Shape Properties

4 Kat describes a quadrilateral.

It has two pairs of equal-length sides.
Its opposite angles are equal, but they are not right angles.
What is the name of this shape?

1 mark

5 Look at this regular pentagon.

Use your knowledge of polygons to work out:

the length of side m.

cm

1 mark

the size of angle v.

°

1 mark

108°

m

7 cm

v

Not to scale

6 Look at the shape below.

Use your knowledge of quadrilaterals to work out:

the length of side q.

cm

1 mark

86°

3 cm

q

116°

a

the length of side r.

cm

1 mark

r

4.5 cm

42°

Not to scale

the size of angle a.

°

1 mark

"I know the properties of different shapes."

Circles

1 Draw an arrow pointing to the circumference of the circle below.

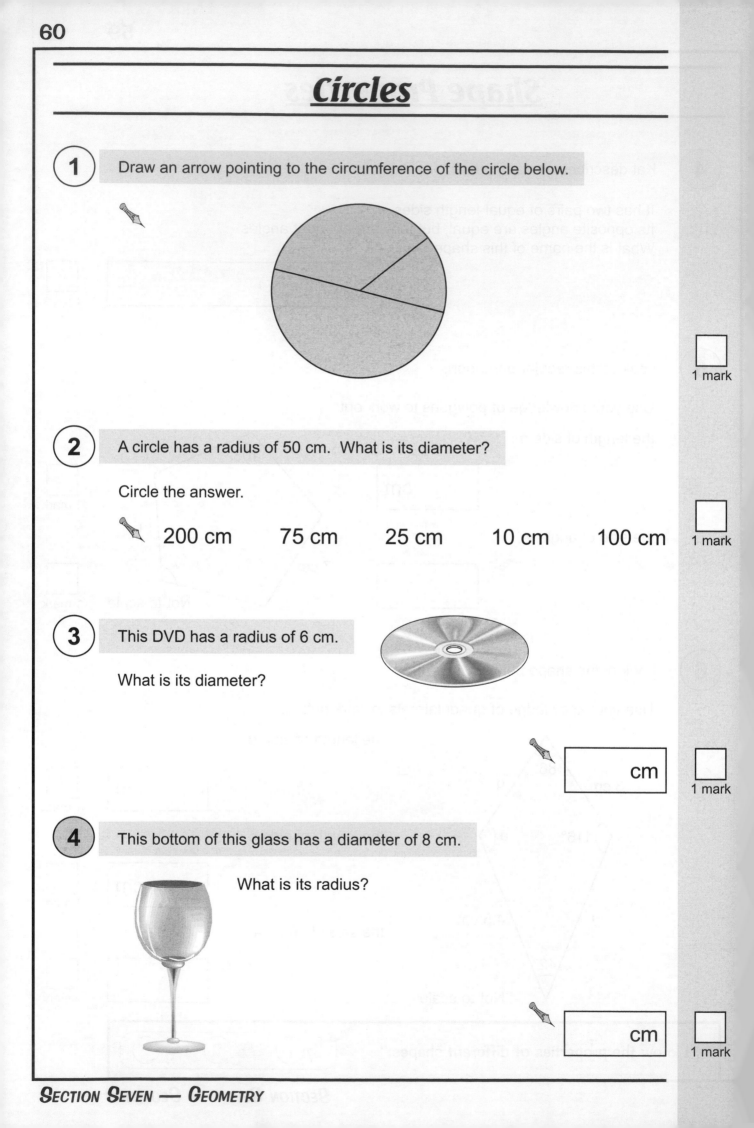

1 mark

2 A circle has a radius of 50 cm. What is its diameter?

Circle the answer.

200 cm   75 cm   25 cm   10 cm   100 cm

1 mark

3 This DVD has a radius of 6 cm.

What is its diameter?

[ ] cm

1 mark

4 This bottom of this glass has a diameter of 8 cm.

What is its radius?

[ ] cm

1 mark

Circles

5 This bike wheel has a diameter of 70 cm.

What is its radius?

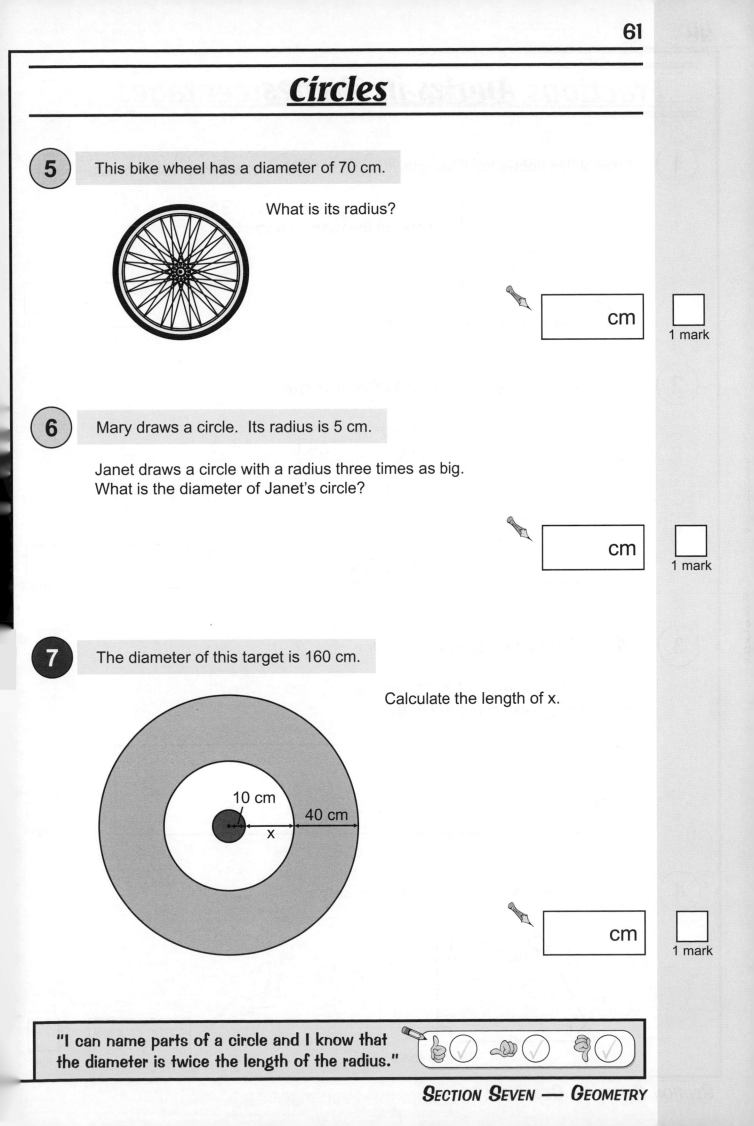

cm

1 mark

6 Mary draws a circle. Its radius is 5 cm.

Janet draws a circle with a radius three times as big.
What is the diameter of Janet's circle?

cm

1 mark

7 The diameter of this target is 160 cm.

Calculate the length of x.

10 cm

40 cm

x

cm

1 mark

"I can name parts of a circle and I know that
the diameter is twice the length of the radius."

SECTION SEVEN — GEOMETRY

Angles in Shapes

1 Look at this right-angled triangle.

54°

90

B

Without using a protractor,
work out the value of angle B.

$$\begin{array}{r} 90 \\ +54 \\ \hline 144 \end{array}$$

36 °

1 mark

2 Find the size of angle x in the quadrilateral below.

42°

x

247°

51°

Not to scale

$$\begin{array}{r} 247 \\ +42 \\ \hline 289 \end{array}$$

$$\begin{array}{r} 289 \\ +\ 51 \\ \hline 340 \end{array}$$

20 °

1 mark

3 Max measures the angles in a triangle.

He says the angles are 50°, 35° and 85°.
Explain why Max cannot be correct.

Triangles have a total of 180° So Max
Cannot be correct

1 mark

4 Find the size of angle t in the trapezium below.

102°

90

t

90

Not to scale

$$\begin{array}{r} 102 \\ +180 \\ \hline 282 \end{array}$$

$$\begin{array}{r} 360 \\ -282 \\ \hline 078 \end{array}$$

78 °

1 mark

Angles in Shapes

5 | Look at this isosceles triangle.

e

46°

f

Calculate the size of angles e and f.

$\begin{array}{r} 1^{7}\cancel{8}^{1}0 \\ -46 \\ \hline 134 \end{array}$

$\begin{array}{r} 067 \\ 2\overline{)134} \end{array}$

e = 67 °   f = 67 °

2 marks

6 | Look at this regular octagon.

What is the sum of its exterior angles?

360

~~360~~48 °

1 mark

Calculate the size of one of its exterior angles.

~~48~~ °

1 mark

7 | A decagon is a 10-sided shape.

Work out the size of one exterior angle of a regular decagon.

~~36~~ °

1 mark

Work out the size of one interior angle of a regular decagon.

~~36~~36 °

1 mark

"I can use my knowledge of shapes to find missing angles."

Angle Rules

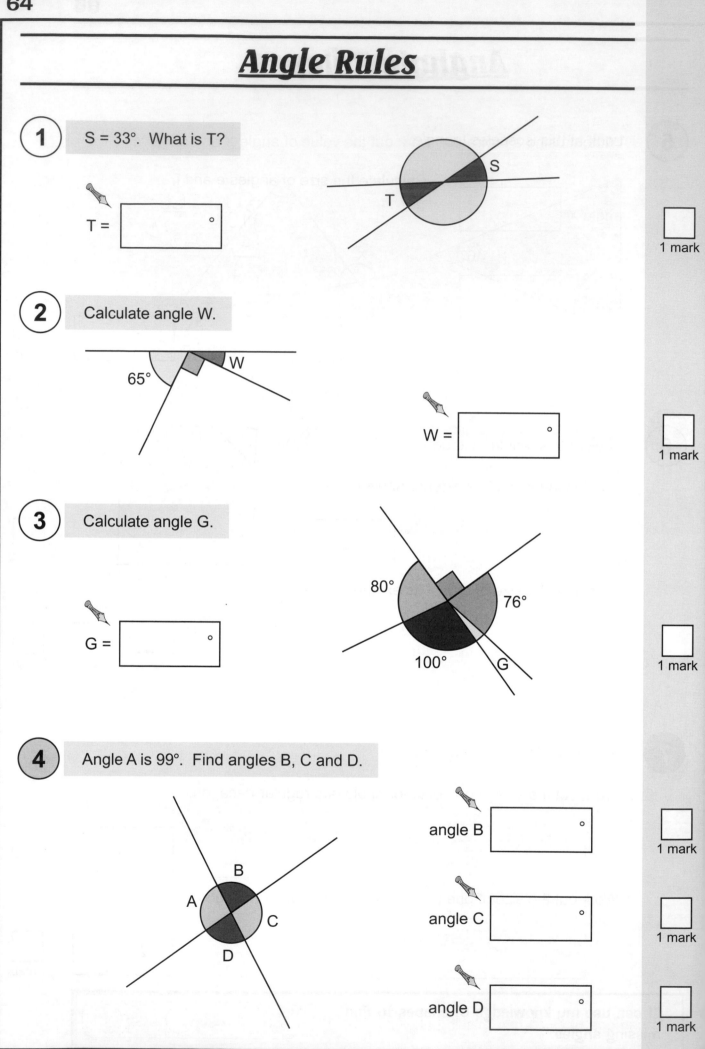

1 S = 33°. What is T?

T = ☐ °

1 mark

2 Calculate angle W.

65°   W

W = ☐ °

1 mark

3 Calculate angle G.

80°   76°

100°   G

G = ☐ °

1 mark

4 Angle A is 99°. Find angles B, C and D.

B

A   C

D

angle B ☐ °

1 mark

angle C ☐ °

1 mark

angle D ☐ °

1 mark

Angle Rules

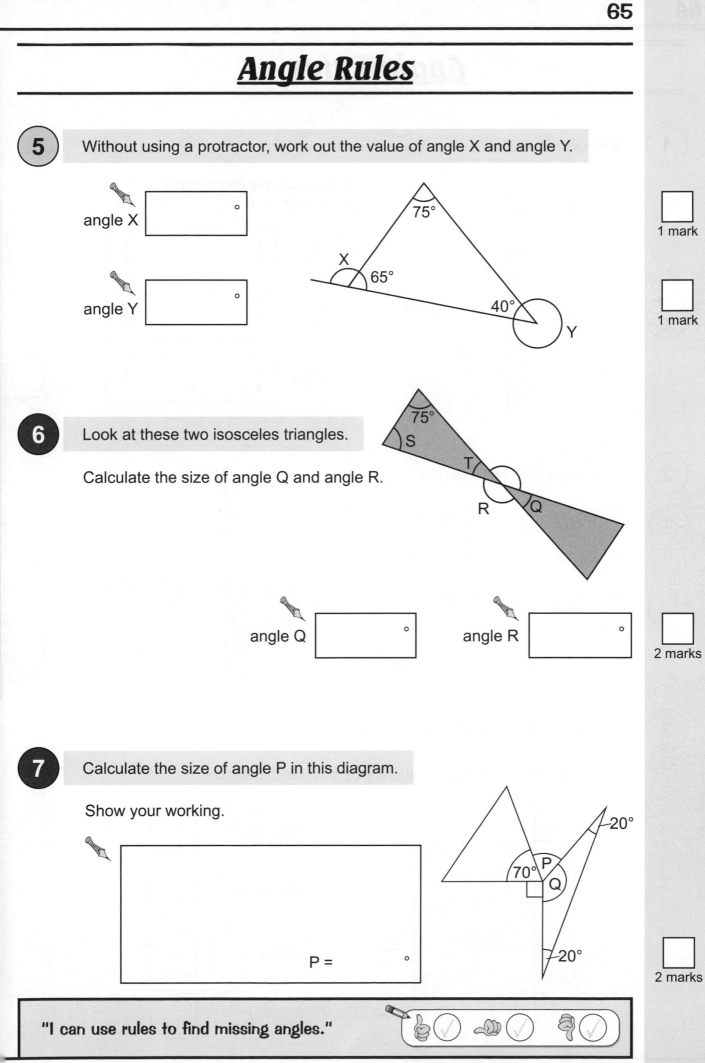

5 Without using a protractor, work out the value of angle X and angle Y.

angle X [___]°

angle Y [___]°

75°

X 65°

40°

Y

1 mark

1 mark

6 Look at these two isosceles triangles.

Calculate the size of angle Q and angle R.

75°

S

T

R Q

angle Q [___]°

angle R [___]°

2 marks

7 Calculate the size of angle P in this diagram.

Show your working.

P = [___]°

70° P

Q

20°

20°

2 marks

"I can use rules to find missing angles."

Coordinates

1 Mel has plotted some coordinates on this grid.

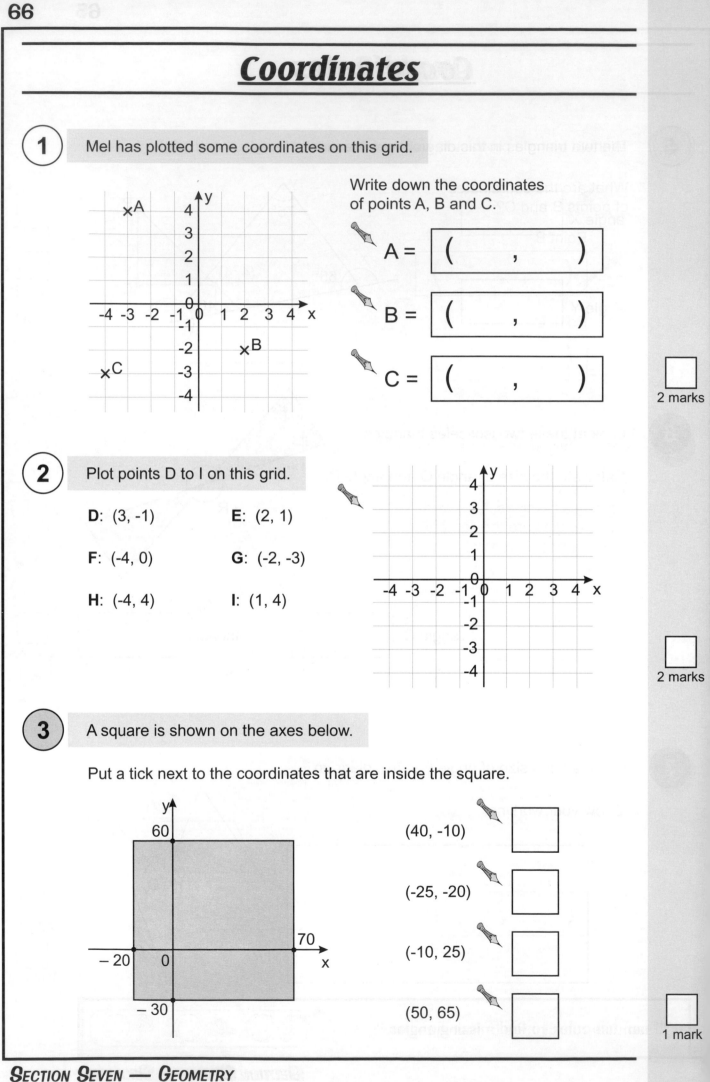

Write down the coordinates of points A, B and C.

A = (,)

B = (,)

C = (,)

2 marks

2 Plot points D to I on this grid.

D: (3, -1)   **E**: (2, 1)

F: (-4, 0)   **G**: (-2, -3)

H: (-4, 4)   **I**: (1, 4)

2 marks

3 A square is shown on the axes below.

Put a tick next to the coordinates that are inside the square.

(40, -10)

(-25, -20)

(-10, 25)

(50, 65)

1 mark

Coordinates

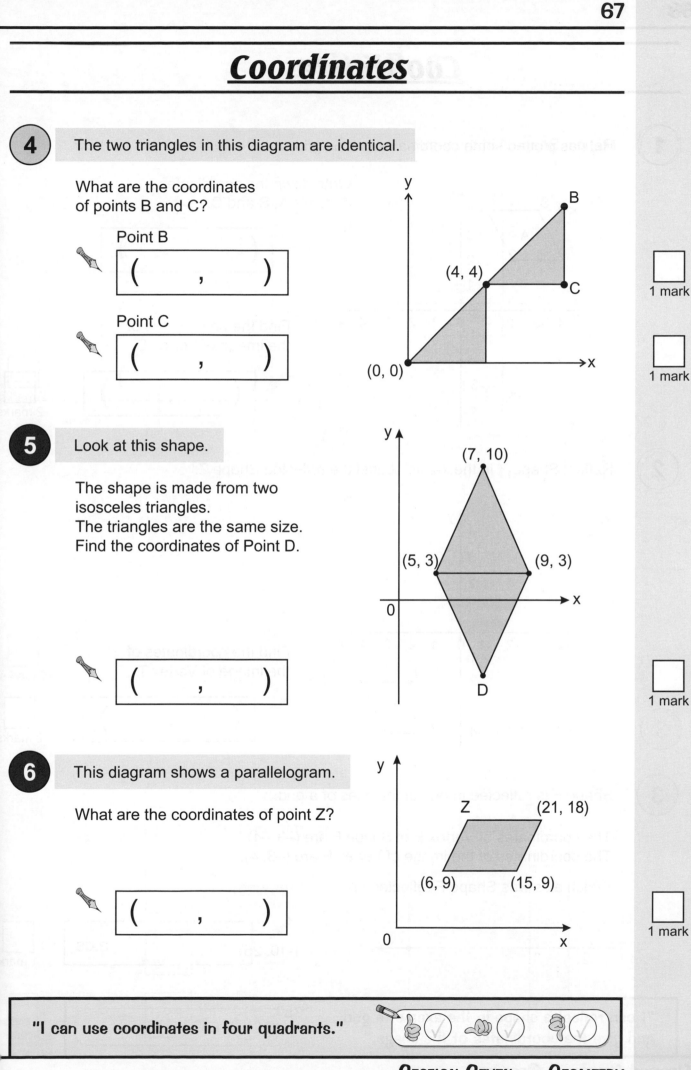

4 The two triangles in this diagram are identical.

What are the coordinates
of points B and C?

Point B

(,   )

1 mark

Point C

(,   )

1 mark

B

(4, 4)

C

(0, 0)

5 Look at this shape.

The shape is made from two
isosceles triangles.
The triangles are the same size.
Find the coordinates of Point D.

(,   )

1 mark

(7, 10)

(5, 3)   (9, 3)

0

D

6 This diagram shows a parallelogram.

What are the coordinates of point Z?

(,   )

1 mark

Z   (21, 18)

(6, 9)   (15, 9)

0

"I can use coordinates in four quadrants."

Reflection

1 Reflect Shape A in the y-axis. Label the reflected Shape B.

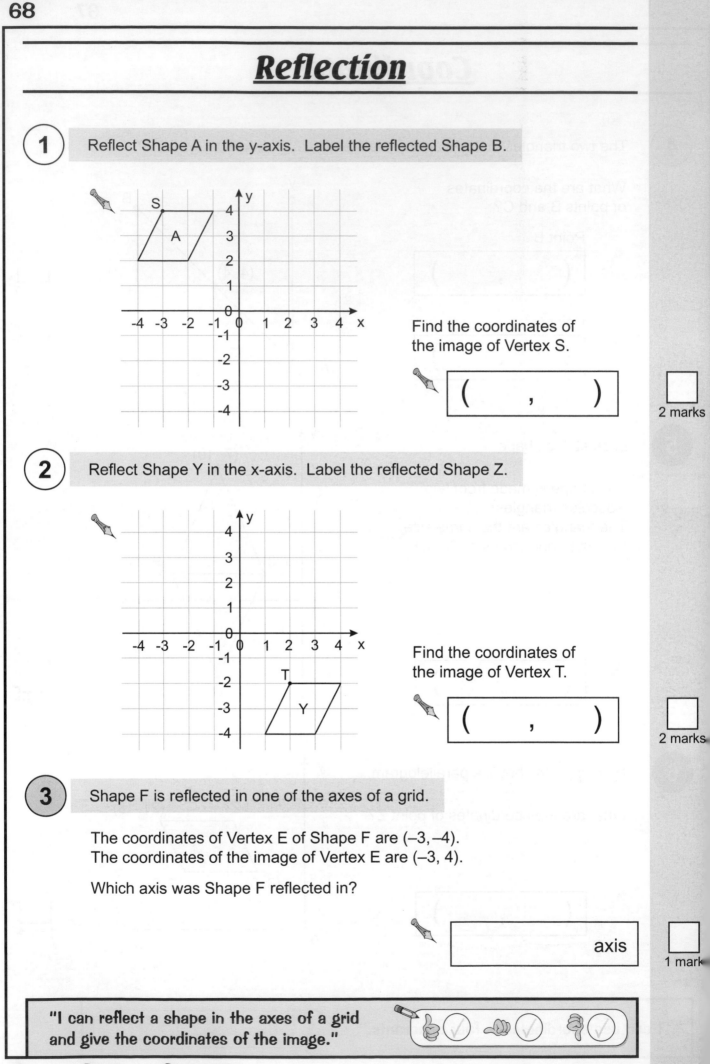

Find the coordinates of
the image of Vertex S.

(,   )

2 marks

2 Reflect Shape Y in the x-axis. Label the reflected Shape Z.

Find the coordinates of
the image of Vertex T.

(,   )

2 marks

3 Shape F is reflected in one of the axes of a grid.

The coordinates of Vertex E of Shape F are (–3, –4).
The coordinates of the image of Vertex E are (–3, 4).

Which axis was Shape F reflected in?

axis

1 mark

"I can reflect a shape in the axes of a grid
and give the coordinates of the image."

Translation

1 Shape D is shown on the grid below.

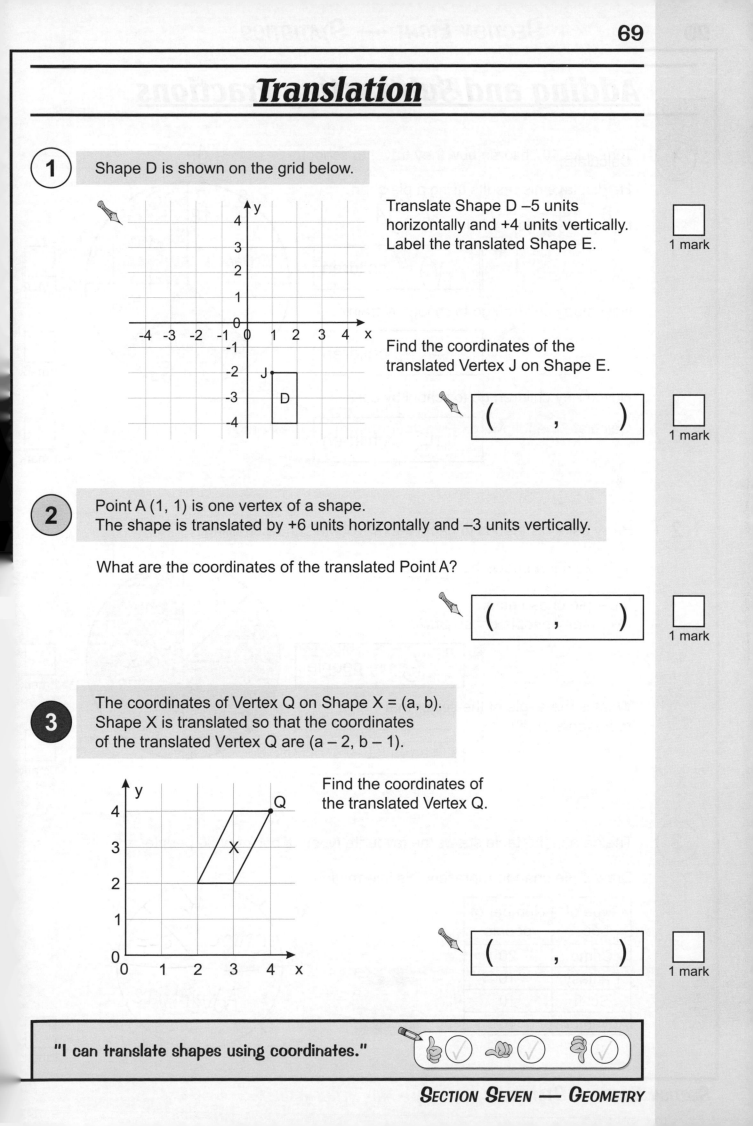

Translate Shape D −5 units horizontally and +4 units vertically. Label the translated Shape E.

Find the coordinates of the translated Vertex J on Shape E.

(,   )

2 Point A (1, 1) is one vertex of a shape.
The shape is translated by +6 units horizontally and −3 units vertically.

What are the coordinates of the translated Point A?

(,   )

3 The coordinates of Vertex Q on Shape X = (a, b).
Shape X is translated so that the coordinates
of the translated Vertex Q are (a − 2, b − 1).

Find the coordinates of
the translated Vertex Q.

(,   )

"I can translate shapes using coordinates."

SECTION SEVEN — GEOMETRY

Pie Charts

1 Tom asks 40 children how they travel to school.

He displays his results using a pie chart.

How many children walk to school?

10 children

1 mark

How many children go to school by train?

5 children

1 mark

How many children go to school by car?

15 children

1 mark

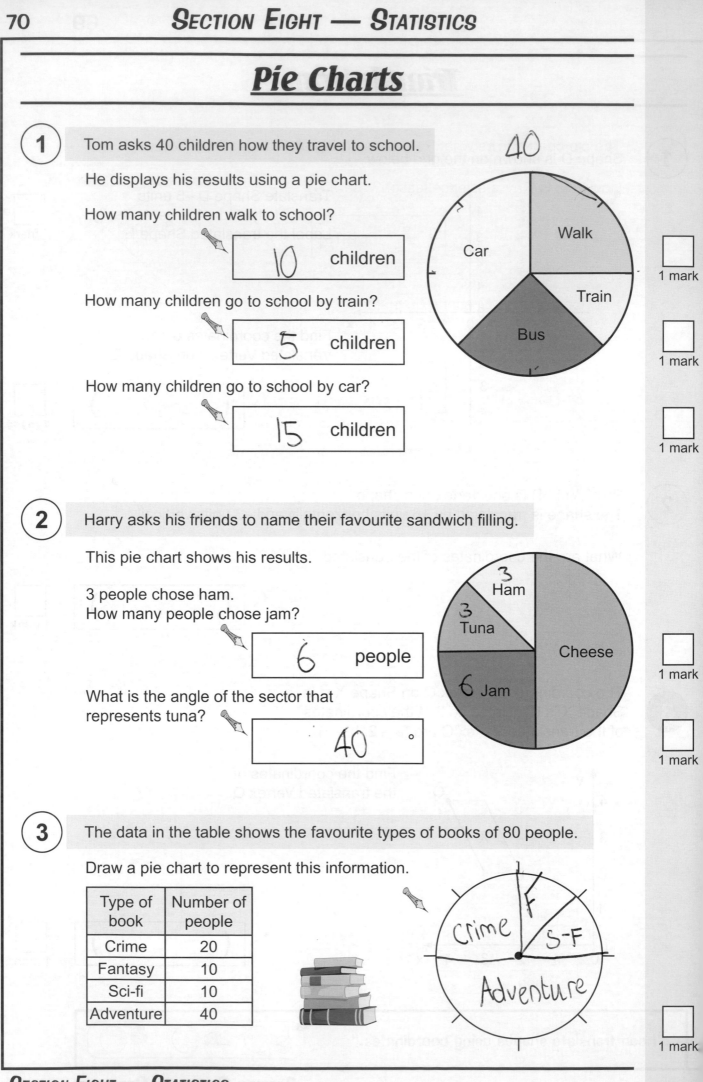

2 Harry asks his friends to name their favourite sandwich filling.

This pie chart shows his results.

3 people chose ham.
How many people chose jam?

6 people

1 mark

What is the angle of the sector that represents tuna?

40 °

1 mark

3 The data in the table shows the favourite types of books of 80 people.

Draw a pie chart to represent this information.

Type of book	Number of people
Crime	20
Fantasy	10
Sci-fi	10
Adventure	40

1 mark

Pie Charts

4 The pie chart shows what Ravi does during an 8-hour school day.

How long is Ravi's science lesson?

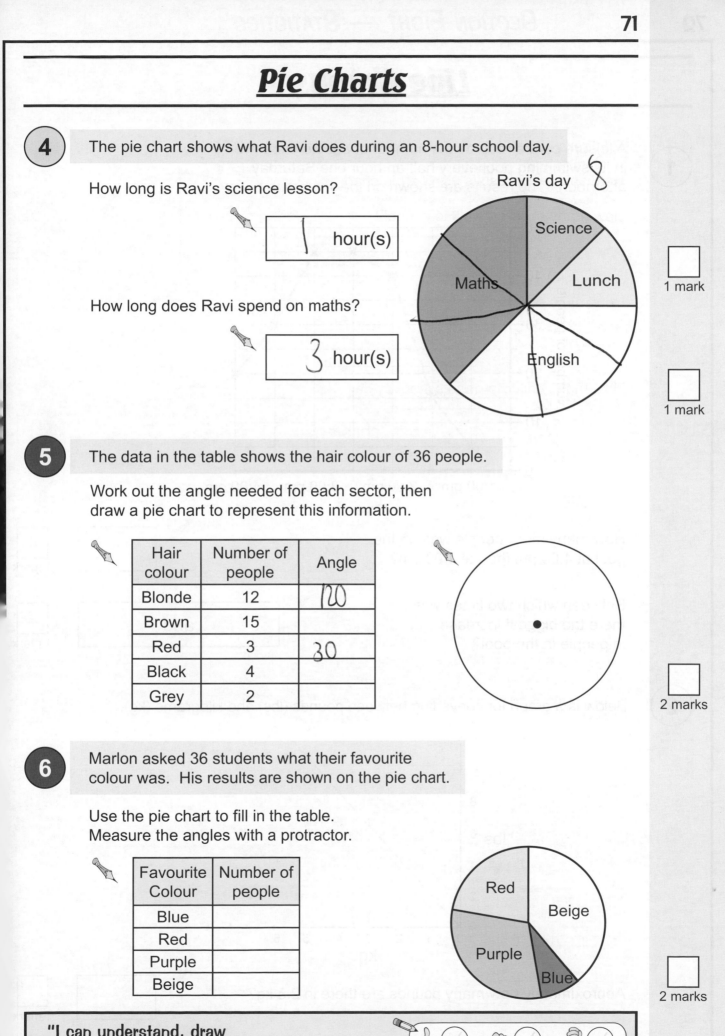

| 1 | hour(s) |

1 mark

How long does Ravi spend on maths?

| 3 | hour(s) |

1 mark

5 The data in the table shows the hair colour of 36 people.

Work out the angle needed for each sector, then draw a pie chart to represent this information.

Hair colour	Number of people	Angle
Blonde	12	120
Brown	15	
Red	3	30
Black	4	
Grey	2	

2 marks

6 Marlon asked 36 students what their favourite colour was. His results are shown on the pie chart.

Use the pie chart to fill in the table.
Measure the angles with a protractor.

Favourite Colour	Number of people
Blue	
Red	
Purple	
Beige	

2 marks

"I can understand, draw and interpret pie charts."

SECTION EIGHT — STATISTICS

Line Graphs

1 A leisure centre records the number of people there are in its swimming pool every half an hour one Saturday afternoon. The results are shown on the line graph below.

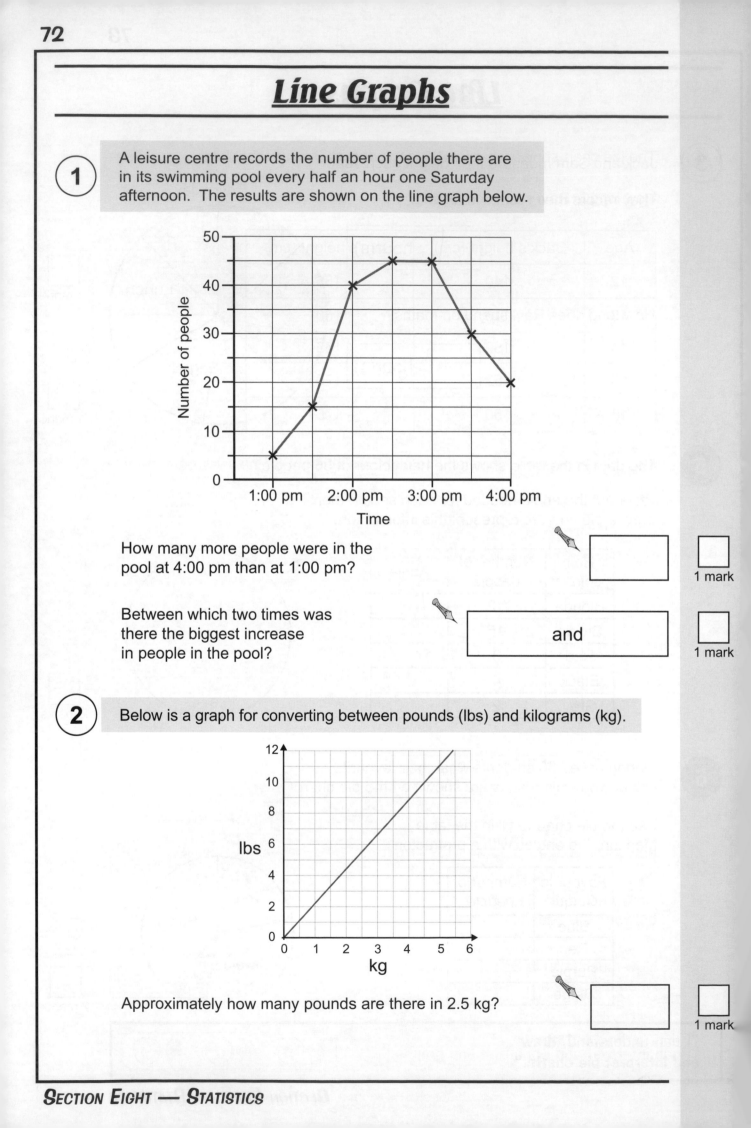

How many more people were in the pool at 4:00 pm than at 1:00 pm?

Between which two times was there the biggest increase in people in the pool?

and

2 Below is a graph for converting between pounds (lbs) and kilograms (kg).

Approximately how many pounds are there in 2.5 kg?

Line Graphs

3 Jack and Sam measure their height each year.

They record their results in a table.

Age	Jack's height (cm)	Sam's height (cm)
12	140	155
13	145	160
14	150	165
15	152	170
16	155	175

Use the information in the table to plot Sam's height on the line graph.

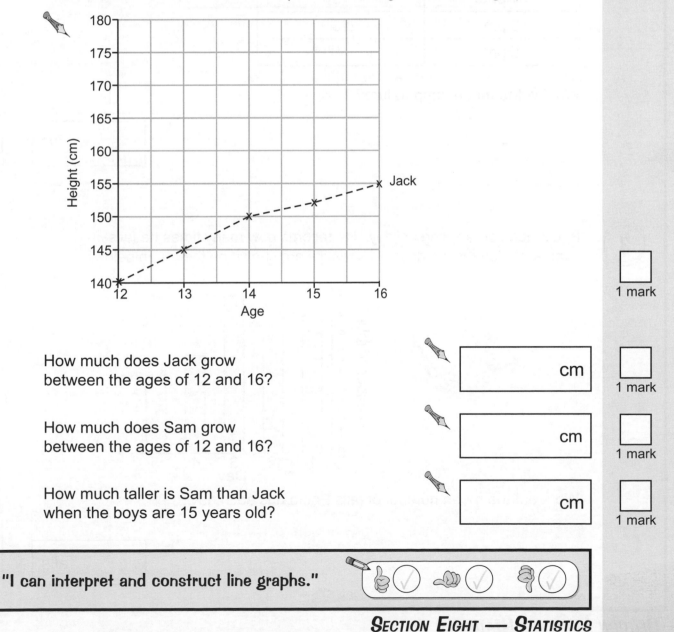

1 mark

How much does Jack grow
between the ages of 12 and 16?

[ ] cm

1 mark

How much does Sam grow
between the ages of 12 and 16?

[ ] cm

1 mark

How much taller is Sam than Jack
when the boys are 15 years old?

[ ] cm

1 mark

"I can interpret and construct line graphs."

The Mean

1 Find the mean of this group of numbers.

$11+10 = 2\sqrt[7]{49}$

7   8   3   6   11   4   10

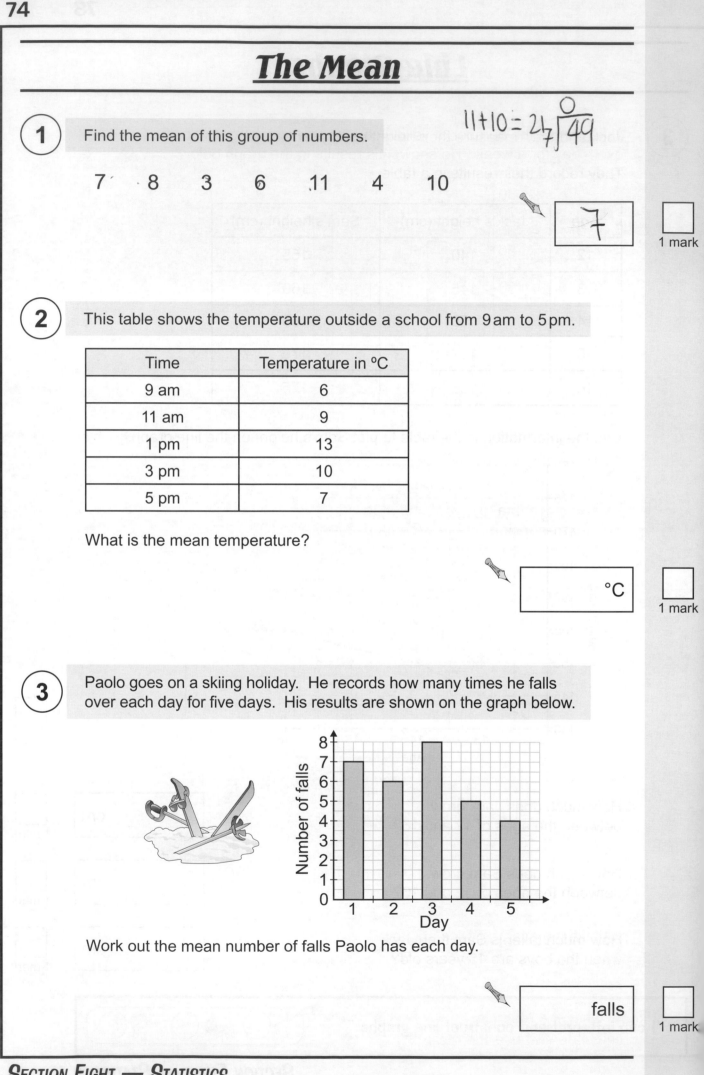

7

1 mark

2 This table shows the temperature outside a school from 9 am to 5 pm.

Time	Temperature in °C
9 am	6
11 am	9
1 pm	13
3 pm	10
5 pm	7

What is the mean temperature?

°C

1 mark

3 Paolo goes on a skiing holiday. He records how many times he falls over each day for five days. His results are shown on the graph below.

Work out the mean number of falls Paolo has each day.

falls

1 mark

The Mean

4 Jake counts the number of yellow cars he sees passing his house every day for a week. He shows his results in the graph below.

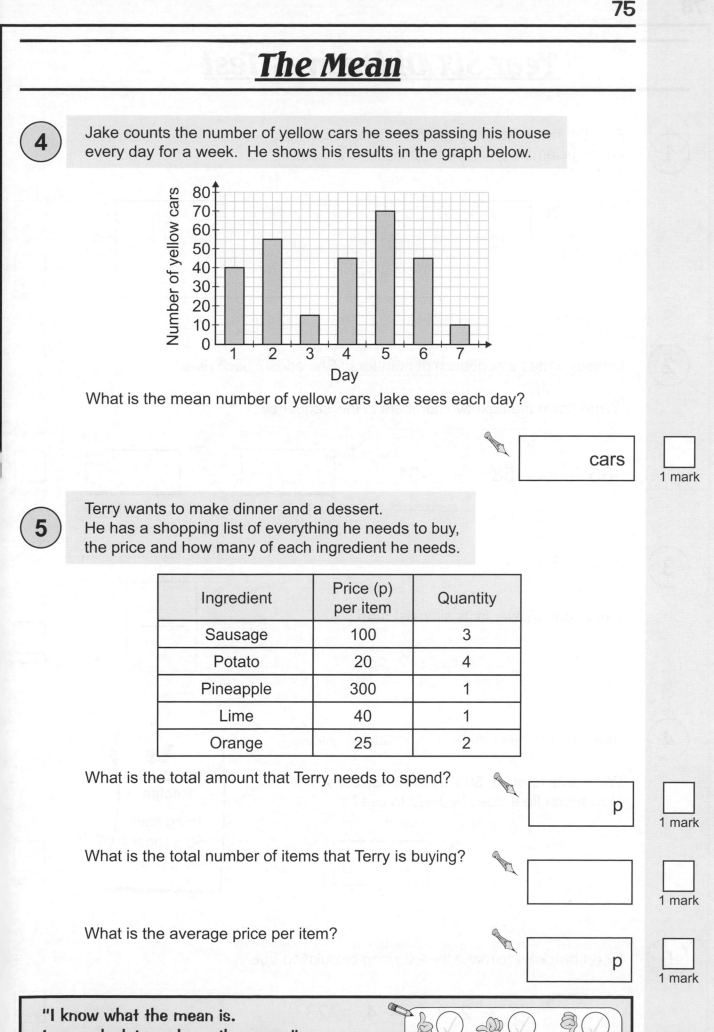

What is the mean number of yellow cars Jake sees each day?

cars

1 mark

5 Terry wants to make dinner and a dessert.
He has a shopping list of everything he needs to buy, the price and how many of each ingredient he needs.

Ingredient	Price (p) per item	Quantity
Sausage	100	3
Potato	20	4
Pineapple	300	1
Lime	40	1
Orange	25	2

What is the total amount that Terry needs to spend?

p

1 mark

What is the total number of items that Terry is buying?

1 mark

What is the average price per item?

p

1 mark

"I know what the mean is.
I can calculate and use the mean."

SECTION EIGHT — STATISTICS

Year Six Objectives Test

1 Which is larger, $\frac{1}{3}$ or $\frac{2}{7}$? Explain how you know.

1 mark

2 Lindsey writes a sequence of numbers. She adds 7 each time.

Write down the next two numbers in this sequence.

-65   -58   -51

1 mark

3 What is $\frac{5}{3} \times \frac{2}{6}$?

Write your answer in its simplest form.

1 mark

4 Here is a recipe to make 12 shortbread biscuits.

Will wants to make 36 shortbread biscuits.
How much flour does he need to use?

[   ] g

Shortbread Recipe

150 g flour
50 g sugar
100 g butter

1 mark

5 Insert brackets to make the following calculation true.

$7 + 2 \times 3 - 4 = 23$

1 mark

6 Enlarge the rectangle shown by a scale factor of 3.

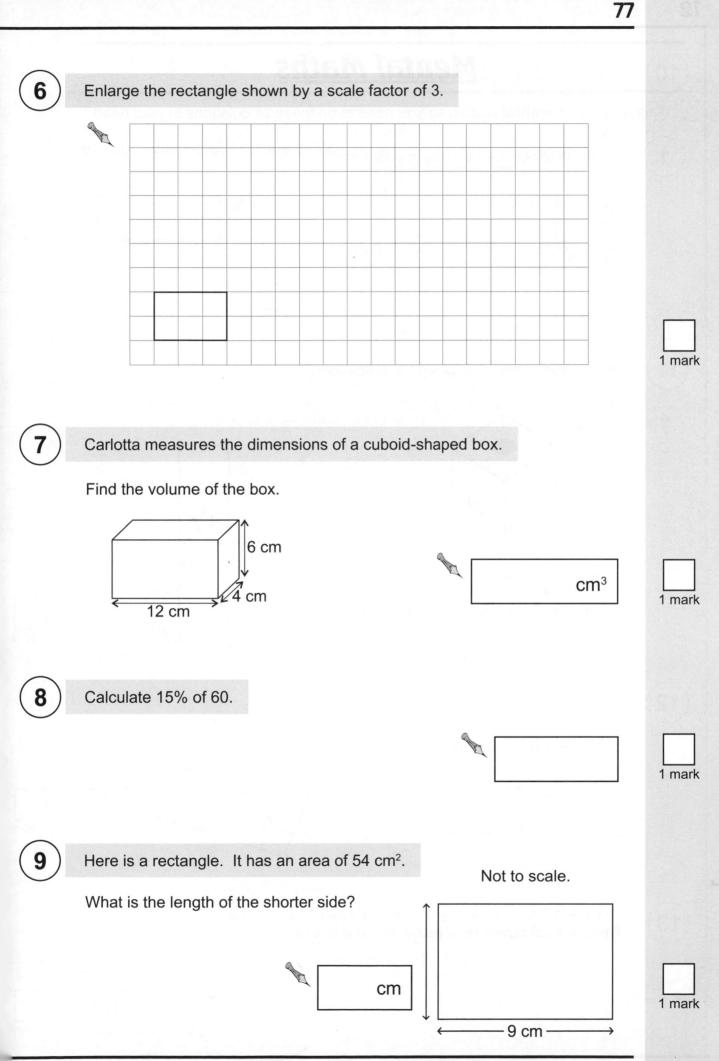

1 mark

7 Carlotta measures the dimensions of a cuboid-shaped box.

Find the volume of the box.

6 cm

4 cm

12 cm

cm³

1 mark

8 Calculate 15% of 60.

1 mark

9 Here is a rectangle. It has an area of 54 cm².

What is the length of the shorter side?

Not to scale.

cm

9 cm

1 mark

10 The shape ABCD is a rectangle.

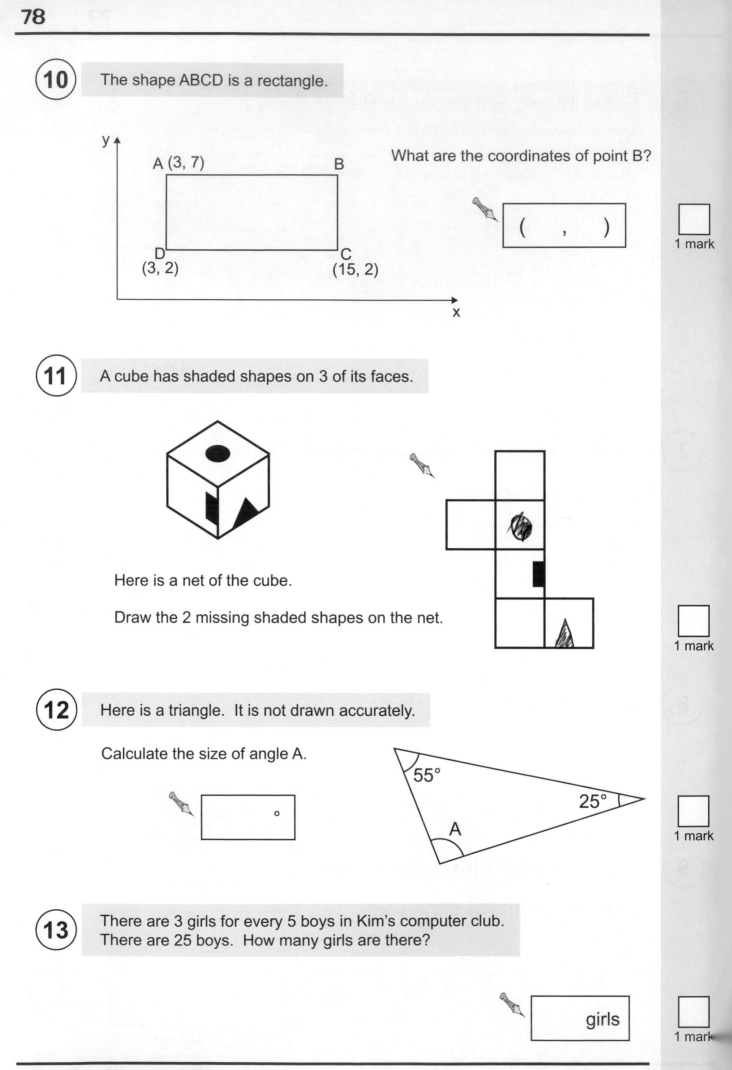

What are the coordinates of point B?

(,   )

1 mark

11 A cube has shaded shapes on 3 of its faces.

Here is a net of the cube.

Draw the 2 missing shaded shapes on the net.

1 mark

12 Here is a triangle. It is not drawn accurately.

Calculate the size of angle A.

°

55°

25°

A

1 mark

13 There are 3 girls for every 5 boys in Kim's computer club.
There are 25 boys. How many girls are there?

girls

1 mark

14 A computer game is sold in-store and online.
In-store it usually costs £25, but has been reduced by 20%.

Online it usually costs £21 but has been reduced by $\frac{1}{3}$.

How much cheaper is it online than in-store?

£ [ ]

2 marks

15 Meg asked each child in her school for their favourite ice cream flavour.
Complete the table and the pie chart below.

Use a protractor to help you.

Flavour	Number of Children	Angle in pie chart
Strawberry	60	120°
Vanilla	40	
Mint	30	
Chocolate	50	

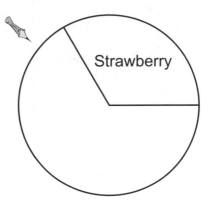

Strawberry

2 marks

16 Calculate 7860 ÷ 12.

2 marks

17 Find the value of M in this equation.

2M + 7 = 25

M = [ ]

1 mark

Total [ ]

Answers

Pages 2-5 — Year Five Objectives Test

Q1

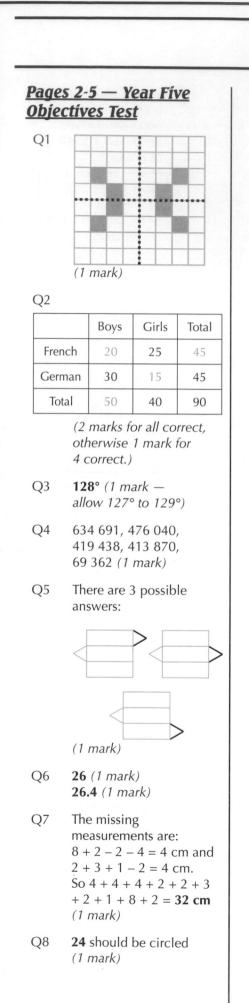

(1 mark)

Q2

	Boys	Girls	Total
French	20	25	45
German	30	15	45
Total	50	40	90

(2 marks for all correct, otherwise 1 mark for 4 correct.)

Q3 **128°** *(1 mark — allow 127° to 129°)*

Q4 634 691, 476 040, 419 438, 413 870, 69 362 *(1 mark)*

Q5 There are 3 possible answers:

(1 mark)

Q6 **26** *(1 mark)*
26.4 *(1 mark)*

Q7 The missing measurements are:
8 + 2 − 2 − 4 = 4 cm and
2 + 3 + 1 − 2 = 4 cm.
So 4 + 4 + 4 + 2 + 2 + 3 + 2 + 1 + 8 + 2 = **32 cm**
(1 mark)

Q8 **24** should be circled
(1 mark)

Q9 One sandwich costs
£3.70 − £2.10 = £1.60.
So one cup of tea costs
£2.10 − £1.60 = £0.50.
So a cup of tea costs **50p**.
(2 marks for correct answer with working, otherwise 1 mark for correct answer only.)

Q10 **64** + **1** = 65 or
1 + **64** = 65 *(1 mark)*

Q11 $\frac{3}{4} = \frac{9}{12}$

$\frac{7}{12} + \frac{9}{12} = \frac{16}{12} = \frac{12}{12} + \frac{4}{12}$

$= 1\frac{4}{12}$ or $1\frac{1}{3}$ *(1 mark)*

Q12
$$7\overline{)2^22^15}\ \ r\,1$$
gives 3 2
32 weeks and 1 day
(1 mark)

Q13
$$\begin{array}{r}4\,5\,6\,0\\-1\,2\,9\,5\\\hline 3\,2\,6\,5\end{array}$$
So she has **3265 g** left.
(1 mark)

Q14 E.g. the patio is made up of two 2 m by 6 m rectangles.
2 × 6 = 12 m²
2 × 12 = **24 m²** *(1 mark)*

Q15 90° + 58° + A = 180°
148° + A = 180°
A = 180° − 148°
A = **32°** *(1 mark)*

Q16 $\frac{3}{5} = \frac{6}{10} = \frac{60}{100} = 60\%$

So **Riley** has eaten the most. *(1 mark)*

Q17
$$\begin{array}{r}1\,2\,5\,5\\\times\ \ \ \ 2\,5\\\hline 6\,2\,7\,5\\+2\,5\,1\,0\,0\\\hline 3\,1\,3\,7\,5\end{array}$$
So she earns **£31 375** in 25 months. *(1 mark)*

Section One — Number and Place Value

Page 6 — Place Value in Very Large Numbers

Q1 **Sixty** *(1 mark)*
Six hundred *(1 mark)*
Six hundred thousand *(1 mark)*

Q2 **72 301 426** *(1 mark)*
Smaller *(1 mark)*

Q3 Smallest: **56 887 206**
65 877 260
65 878 206
65 887 026
Biggest: **65 887 206**
(1 mark)

Page 7 — Rounding Whole Numbers

Q1 **4300** and **4400** *(1 mark)*
4400 *(1 mark)*

Q2 **70 069**, **69 984** and
70 284 should be circled
(1 mark for all correct)
69 984 *(1 mark)*

Q3 **15 473 000** *(1 mark)*
15 470 000 *(1 mark)*
20 000 000 *(1 mark)*

Page 8 — Calculating with Negative Numbers

Q1 **10 °C** *(1 mark)*

Q2 −5 + 7 = **2** *(1 mark)*
−7 + 4 = **−3** *(1 mark)*
−1 − 5 = **−6** *(1 mark)*
1 − 5 = **−4** *(1 mark)*

Q3 **3 °C** *(1 mark)*
8 °C *(1 mark)*

Page 9 — Solving Number Problems

Q1 −27 + 19 = −8, so it is
8 m below the surface.
(1 mark)
−8 to 0 = 8 m
0 to 7 = 7 m
8 + 7 = **15 m** *(1 mark)*

Answers

Q2 **£600** *(1 mark)*
–£100 *(1 mark)*
–117 to 0 is £117.
0 to 631 is £631.
  117
+ 631
  748
So John needs **£748** more.
(1 mark)

Q3 **hundred** *(1 mark)*
thousand *(1 mark)*
million *(1 mark)*

Section Two — Calculations

Page 10 — Written Multiplication

Q1
```
    152
  ×  82
    304
+12160
  12464   (1 mark)
```
```
    238
  ×  37
   1666
 +7140
   8806   (1 mark)
      1
```

Q2
```
    4118
  ×   28
   32944
 +82360
  115304   (1 mark)
     1 1
```
```
    2461
  ×   67
   17227
+147660
  164887   (1 mark)
      1
```

Q3
```
    5631
  ×   92
   11262
+506790
  518052   (1 mark)
     1 1
```

Page 11 — Written Division

Q1
```
        36
   16│576
     -48
       96
      -96
        0   (1 mark)
```

```
       126
   12│1512
     -12
       31
      -24
        72
       -72
         0   (1 mark)
```

Q2
```
       154
   11│1699
     -11
       59
      -55
        49
        44
         5   (1 mark)
```
154 remainder 5, which is **154⁵/₁₁**. *(1 mark)*

```
       555
   16│8888
     -80
       88
      -80
        88
       -80
         8   (1 mark)
```
555 remainder 8, which is **555½** (allow any fraction equivalent to a half). *(1 mark)*

Q3
```
       137
   15│2058
     -15
       55
      -45
       108
       105
         3   (1 mark)
```
There will be 137 full tables and one table with 3 people. So they need **138 tables.** *(1 mark)*
15 – 3 = **12 empty seats.** *(1 mark)*

Page 12 — Mental Maths

Q1 3030 = 3000 + 30
4321 + 3000 = 7321
7321 + 30 = **7351**
(1 mark)

2460 = 2000 + 400 + 60
8000 – 2000 = 6000
6000 – 400 = 5600
5600 – 60 = **5540**
(1 mark)
Make 1200 a hundred times smaller: 12.
12 × 12 = 144
144 × 100 = **14 400**
(1 mark)

Q2 99 500 = 90 000 + 9 000 + 500
383 000 – 90 000 = 293 000
293 000 – 9000 = 284 000
284 000 – 500 = **283 500 km** *(1 mark)*

Q3 58 = 50 + 8
50 ÷ 2 = 25
8 ÷ 2 = 4
25 + 4 = 29
29 – 11 = **18 years old**
(1 mark)

17 = 10 + 7
58 – 10 = 48
48 – 7 = 41
41 = 40 + 1
40 × 2 = 80
1 × 2 = 2
80 + 2 = **82 years old**
(1 mark)

Q4 10 911 + 8848
8848 = 8000 + 800 + 40 + 8
10 911 + 8000 = 18 911
18 911 + 800 = 19 711
19 711 + 40 = 19 751
19 751 + 8 = **19 759 m**
(1 mark)

Page 13 — Estimating and Checking

Q1 21.29 × 38 = 809.02 is about the same as **20 × 40 = 800**. *(1 mark)*

Q2 28.33 × 6 is about the same as 30 × 6 = **180**. *(1 mark)*

Answers

Q3   27.7 lies between 25 and 30. $25 \div 5 = 5$, and $30 \div 5 = 6$. So $27.7 \div 5$ is somewhere between **5** and **6**. *(1 mark)*

Q4 2.89×5280 is about the same as $3 \times 5000 =$ **15 000 feet**. *(1 mark)*

Page 14 — BODMAS

Q1 $12 \div 4 + 2 = $ **5** *(1 mark)*
$8 \times (3 - 1) = $ **16** *(1 mark)*
$5 \times 3 - 5 = $ **10** *(1 mark)*

Q2 $(6 + 6) \times 3 - 3 = 33$ *(1 mark)*
$(2 + 5) \times (7 - 3) = 28$ *(1 mark)*

Q3   Work out the brackets first — $(4 - 2) = 2$
Then the division —
$12 \div 2 = 6$
Then the multiplication —
$6 \times 3 = $ **18** *(1 mark)*

Q4   **(4 × 9) ÷ (1 + 5)** should be circled. *(1 mark)*
$(4 \times 9) \div (1 + 5) = $ **6 slices**. *(1 mark)*

Page 15 — Multiples, Factors and Primes

Q1   **36** *(1 mark)*

Q2   Any three of: **1**, **2**, **3**, **4**, **6**, **12** *(1 mark)*

Q3   **11**, **31**, **41**, **61** and **71** should be circled *(1 mark for all correct)*

Q4 $2 \times 3 \times 11 = 66$ — the numbers may be in any order *(1 mark)*

Q5   There are ten multiples of three: 3, 6, 9, 12, 15, 18, 21, 24, 27, 30.
There are six multiples of five: 5, 10, 15, 20, 25, 30.
There are two multiples of both three and five: 15, 30.

15 and 30 are worth £5, so count them separately.
$8 + 4 + (2 \times 5) = $ **£22**
(2 marks for the correct answer, otherwise 1 mark for giving the multiples of 3 and 5.)

Pages 16-17 — Solving Calculation Problems

Q1 $36 + 18 = 54$
$54 - 24 = $ **30** *(1 mark)*

Q2 $5 + 6 + 4 = 15$ sacks.
$15 \times 10 = $ **150 balls** *(1 mark)*
$15 - 2 - 1 = 12$ sacks left. $12 \times 10 = $ **120 balls** *(1 mark)*

Q3 $4 \times 12 = 48$ sweets.
$48 \div 8 = $ **6 sweets** each *(1 mark)*

Q4 $4 + 5 = 9$ litres used.
Each tin contains 3 litres, $9 \div 3 = 3$, so he needs **3 tins**. *(1 mark)*
Started with $6 \times 3 = 18$ litres of paint.
$18 - 9 = 9$ litres.
Yes, he has enough.
(1 mark)

Q5 $23 + 7 = 30$. $30 \div 2 = $ **15 years old** *(1 mark)*

Q6 $3 \times 7 = 21$. $21 \times 2 = 42$. $60 - 42 = $ **18 litres** *(1 mark)*

Q7 $£5 \times 7 = £35$,
$£3 \times 9 = £27$,
$£2.50 \times 10 = £25$.
Rebecca made:
$35 + 27 + 25 = £87$.
$87 - 15 - 21 = $ **£51**
(2 marks for the correct answer, otherwise 1 mark for £87.)

Q8 $5 \times 10 = 50$. With five pieces of rope, there will be four overlaps.
$4 \times 0.5 = 2$
$50 - 2 = $ **48 m** *(1 mark)*

Section Three — Fractions, Decimals and Percentages

Page 18 — Simplifying Fractions

Q1 $12 \div 4 = 3$, $16 \div 4 = 4$
so $\dfrac{12}{16} = \dfrac{3}{4}$ *(1 mark)*
$20 \div 5 = 4$, $25 \div 5 = 5$
so $\dfrac{20}{25} = \dfrac{4}{5}$ *(1 mark)*
$12 \div 12 = 1$, $72 \div 12 = 6$
so $\dfrac{12}{72} = \dfrac{1}{6}$ *(1 mark)*
$33 \div 11 = 3$,
$121 \div 11 = 11$
so $\dfrac{33}{121} = \dfrac{3}{11}$ *(1 mark)*

Q2 $\dfrac{30}{50}$, $\dfrac{45}{75}$ and $\dfrac{24}{40}$ should be circled. *(1 mark for all correct)*

Q3 $\dfrac{5}{15}$ and $\dfrac{27}{81}$ should be circled. *(1 mark for both correct)*

Q4   E.g. $1 \times 4 = 4$
$6 \times 4 = 24$
So $\dfrac{1}{6} = \dfrac{4}{24}$

$3 \times 3 = 9$
$8 \times 3 = 24$
So $\dfrac{3}{8} = \dfrac{9}{24}$
(2 marks for 2 correct equivalent fractions with the same denominator, otherwise 1 mark for one correct equivalent fraction.)

Page 19 — Ordering Fractions

Q1   Make equivalent fractions with the same denominator:
$\dfrac{1}{2} = \dfrac{10}{20}$, $\dfrac{3}{5} = \dfrac{12}{20}$
and $\dfrac{4}{20}$

Answers

So the order is:
$\frac{4}{20}, \frac{1}{2}, \frac{3}{5}$ *(1 mark)*

Q2 Make equivalent fractions with the same denominator:
$\frac{2}{3} = \frac{10}{15}, \frac{4}{5} = \frac{12}{15}$ and $\frac{8}{15}$

So the order is:
$\frac{4}{5}, \frac{2}{3}, \frac{8}{15}$ *(1 mark)*

Q3 $1\frac{7}{8} = \frac{15}{8}$
$2\frac{1}{8} = \frac{8+8+1}{8} = \frac{17}{8}$
So the order is:
$\frac{12}{8}, \frac{14}{8}, 1\frac{7}{8}, 2\frac{1}{8}$ *(1 mark)*

Q4 Make equivalent fractions with the same denominator:
$\frac{5}{3} = \frac{50}{30}, \frac{6}{5} = \frac{36}{30},$
$\frac{3}{2} = \frac{45}{30}$ and $\frac{7}{6} = \frac{35}{30}$

So the order is:
$= \frac{7}{6}, \frac{6}{5}, \frac{3}{2}, \frac{5}{3}$ *(1 mark)*

Pages 20-21 — Adding and Subtracting Fractions

Q1 $\frac{1}{4} = \frac{2}{8}, \frac{1}{8} + \frac{2}{8} = \frac{1+2}{8}$
$= \frac{3}{8}$ *(1 mark)*
$\frac{3}{7} = \frac{6}{14}, \frac{6}{14} - \frac{3}{14} = \frac{6-3}{14}$
$= \frac{3}{14}$ *(1 mark)*
$\frac{8}{9} = \frac{16}{18},$
$\frac{16}{18} - \frac{3}{18} = \frac{16-3}{18} = \frac{13}{18}$
(1 mark)

Q2 $\frac{2}{5} = \frac{12}{30}, \frac{1}{3} = \frac{10}{30},$
$\frac{3}{6} = \frac{15}{30}$
$\frac{12}{30} + \frac{10}{30} - \frac{15}{30}$
$= \frac{12+10-15}{30} = \frac{7}{30}$
(1 mark)

$\frac{2}{3} = \frac{8}{12}, \frac{1}{4} = \frac{3}{12},$
$\frac{2}{6} = \frac{4}{12}$
$\frac{8}{12} - \frac{3}{12} + \frac{4}{12}$
$= \frac{8-3+4}{12} = \frac{9}{12} = \frac{3}{4}$
(1 mark)

Q3 Make equivalent fractions:
$\frac{5}{6} = \frac{20}{24}, \frac{7}{8} = \frac{21}{24}$
Two cakes $= \frac{48}{24}$
$\frac{48}{24} - \frac{20}{24} - \frac{21}{24} = \frac{48-20-21}{24}$
$= \frac{7}{24}$ *(1 mark)*
$\frac{2}{9} = \frac{4}{18}, \frac{2}{6} = \frac{6}{18}$
One bowl of sweets $= \frac{18}{18}$
$\frac{18}{18} - \frac{4}{18} - \frac{6}{18} = \frac{8}{18}$ or $\frac{4}{9}$
(1 mark)

Q4 $4\frac{6}{11} = \frac{50}{11} = \frac{100}{22}$
$\frac{100}{22} + \frac{7}{22} = \frac{100+7}{22} = \frac{107}{22}$
$= 4\frac{19}{22}$ *(1 mark)*

$\frac{35}{12} = \frac{70}{24}, 1\frac{5}{8} = \frac{13}{8} = \frac{39}{24}$
$\frac{70}{24} - \frac{39}{24} = \frac{70-39}{24} = \frac{31}{24}$
$= 1\frac{7}{24}$ *(1 mark)*

Q5 $7\frac{6}{8} = \frac{62}{8} = \frac{31}{4}$
$25 + ? = 31$
$25 + 6 = 31$
So $\frac{25}{4} + \frac{6}{4} = 7\frac{6}{8}$
(1 mark)

$2\frac{2}{11} = \frac{24}{11} = \frac{48}{22},$
$\frac{14}{11} = \frac{28}{22}$
$48 - ? = 28$
$48 - 20 = 28$
So $2\frac{2}{11} - \frac{20}{22} = \frac{14}{11}$
(1 mark)

Q6 $\frac{18}{5} + \frac{4}{3} = \frac{54}{15} + \frac{20}{15} = \frac{74}{15}$
$\frac{12}{10} - \frac{1}{3} = \frac{36}{30} - \frac{10}{30} = \frac{26}{30}$
$2\frac{1}{2} + \frac{7}{3} = \frac{5}{2} + \frac{7}{3}$
$= \frac{15}{6} + \frac{14}{6} = \frac{29}{6}$
$\frac{74}{15} = \frac{148}{30}, \frac{29}{6} = \frac{145}{30}$
So $\frac{148}{30} = \frac{18}{5} + \frac{4}{3}$
gives the largest fraction
(2 marks for the correct answer, otherwise 1 mark for $\frac{74}{15}, \frac{26}{30}$ and $\frac{29}{6}$).

Page 22 — Multiplying Fractions

Q1 $\frac{1}{3} \times \frac{1}{5} = \frac{1}{15}$ *(1 mark)*
$\frac{1}{4} \times \frac{1}{9} = \frac{1}{36}$ *(1 mark)*

Q2 $\frac{1}{3} \times \frac{3}{4} = \frac{3}{12} = \frac{1}{4}$ *(1 mark)*

Q3 $\frac{1}{4} \times \frac{2}{5} = \frac{2}{20}$
$\frac{3}{8} \times \frac{4}{5} = \frac{12}{40}$
$\frac{3}{10} \times \frac{2}{3} = \frac{6}{30}$
$\frac{2}{20} = \frac{1}{10}, \frac{6}{30} = \frac{2}{10}$
and $\frac{12}{40} = \frac{3}{10}$
So $\frac{3}{8} \times \frac{4}{5}$ gives the largest fraction.
(2 marks for the correct answer, otherwise 1 mark for $\frac{2}{20}, \frac{12}{40}$ and $\frac{6}{30}$).

Page 23 — Dividing Fractions by Whole Numbers

Q1 $\frac{1}{2} \div 5 = \frac{1}{10}$ *(1 mark)*
$\frac{1}{8} \div 3 = \frac{1}{24}$ *(1 mark)*
$\frac{1}{4} \div 8 = \frac{1}{32}$ *(1 mark)*
$\frac{1}{12} \div 6 = \frac{1}{72}$ *(1 mark)*

Answers

Q2 $\frac{6}{11} \div 3 = \frac{6}{33} = \mathbf{\frac{2}{11}}$
(1 mark)

$\frac{14}{15} \div 4 = \frac{14}{60} = \mathbf{\frac{7}{30}}$
(1 mark)

Q3 $1 - \frac{1}{3} = \frac{2}{3}$
$\frac{2}{3} \div 4 = \frac{2}{12} = \mathbf{\frac{1}{6}}$ *(1 mark)*

Page 24 — Multiplying or Dividing by 10, 100 or 1000

Q1   **8 tenths** *(1 mark)*
80 *(1 mark)*
8 thousandths *(1 mark)*

Q2 $211.2 \div 100 = \mathbf{2.112}$
(1 mark)
$18 \times 1000 = \mathbf{18\ 000}$
(1 mark)

Q3   **100** *(1 mark)*
10 *(1 mark)*
1000 *(1 mark)*

Page 25 — Multiplying with Decimals

Q1 $6 \times 8 = 48$
6 is 10 times larger than 0.6, so divide by 10.
$48 \div 10 = \mathbf{4.8}$ *(1 mark)*
$9 \times 7 = 63$
9 is 100 times larger than 0.09, so divide by 100.
$63 \div 100 = \mathbf{0.63}$ *(1 mark)*

Q2
$$\begin{array}{r} 24 \\ \times \quad 7 \\ \hline 168 \\ {\scriptstyle 2} \end{array}$$
24 is 10 times larger than 2.4, so divide by 10.
$168 \div 10 = \mathbf{16.8}$ *(1 mark)*

$$\begin{array}{r} 618 \\ \times \quad 9 \\ \hline 5\,562 \\ {\scriptstyle 1\ 7} \end{array}$$
618 is 100 times larger than 6.18, so divide by 100. $5562 \div 100 = \mathbf{55.62}$
(1 mark)

Q3
$$\begin{array}{r} 3\,45 \\ \times \quad 7 \\ \hline 2415 \\ {\scriptstyle 3\ 3} \end{array}$$
345 is 100 times larger than 3.45, so divide by 100. $2415 \div 100 =$ **£24.15** *(1 mark)*

$$\begin{array}{r} 410 \\ \times \quad 7 \\ \hline 2870 \end{array}$$
410 is 100 times larger than 4.10, so divide by 100.
$2870 \div 100 = £28.70$
$£28.70 - £24.15 = \mathbf{£4.55}$
(1 mark)

Page 26 — Dividing with Decimals

Q1 $9 \div 3 = 3$
9 is 100 times larger than 0.09, so divide by 100.
$3 \div 100 = \mathbf{0.03}$ *(1 mark)*
$12 \div 6 = 2$
12 is 100 times larger than 0.12, so divide by 100.
$2 \div 100 = \mathbf{0.02}$ *(1 mark)*

Q2   Calculate $1008 \div 8$ first.
$$\begin{array}{r} 0\,1\,2\,6 \\ 8\,\overline{)1^10^20^48} \end{array}$$
1008 is 100 times larger than 10.08, so divide by 100. $126 \div 100 = \mathbf{1.26}$
(1 mark)
Calculate $2064 \div 6$ first.
$$\begin{array}{r} 0\,3\,4\,4 \\ 6\,\overline{)2^20^26^24} \end{array}$$
2064 is 10 times larger than 206.4, so divide by 10. $344 \div 10 = \mathbf{34.4}$
(1 mark)

Q3 $£3.87 = 387p.$
$$\begin{array}{r} 0\,4\,3 \\ 9\,\overline{)3^38^27} \end{array}$$
$43p = \mathbf{£0.43}$ *(1 mark)*

Q4   Calculate $1288 \div 8$ first.
$$\begin{array}{r} 0\,1\,6\,1 \\ 8\,\overline{)1^12^48\,8} \end{array}$$
1288 is 10 times bigger than 128.8, so divide by 10. $161 \div 10 = \mathbf{16.1\ cm}$
(1 mark)

Page 27 — Rounding Decimals

Q1   **2.61**, **2.59**, **2.56**, **2.55** and **2.60** should be circled.
(1 mark for all correct)

Q2   11.23 rounds to **11.2**
0.09 rounds to **0.1**
3.456 rounds to **3.5**
(2 marks for all correct, otherwise 1 mark for 2 correct.)

Q3   14.282 rounds to **14.28**
0.215 rounds to **0.22**
27.595 rounds to **27.60**
(2 marks for all correct, otherwise 1 mark for 2 correct.)

Q4   **13.018** and **12.956** should be circled.
(1 mark)

Q5   **4.361**, **4.362**, **4.363**, **4.364** *(1 mark)*

Pages 28-29 — Fractions, Decimals and Percentages

Q1 $0.66 = \frac{66}{100}$

$67\% = \frac{67}{100}$

$\frac{34}{50} = \frac{68}{100}$

So the order is:
$\mathbf{0.66}$, $\mathbf{67\%}$, $\mathbf{\frac{34}{50}}$, $\mathbf{\frac{69}{100}}$
(1 mark)

Q2 $\frac{3}{5} = \frac{60}{100} = 0.6$,
so **0.65 is bigger** *(1 mark)*
$\frac{37}{50} = \frac{74}{100} = 74\%$
so $\mathbf{\frac{37}{50}}$ **is bigger** *(1 mark)*
$\frac{3}{25} = \frac{12}{100} = 0.12$
so **0.15 is bigger** *(1 mark)*
$\frac{9}{25} = \frac{36}{100} = 0.36$
so **0.38 is bigger** *(1 mark)*

Q3 $0.44 = \frac{44}{100} = \mathbf{\frac{11}{25}}$ *(1 mark)*
$= \mathbf{44\%}$ *(1 mark)*

Answers

$0.8 = \frac{80}{100} = \frac{20}{25}$ *(1 mark)*
$= \mathbf{80\%}$ *(1 mark)*

Q4 **Mr Jukes**. E.g. $\frac{19}{25} = \frac{76}{100}$
$= 76\%$, which is greater
than 75% *(1 mark)*

Q5 $\frac{4}{40} = 10\%$, $0.02 = 2\%$,
$\frac{2}{20} = 10\%$, $\frac{4}{20} = 20\%$,
$0.2 = 20\%$ and $\frac{2}{5} = 40\%$.
So the equivalent
amounts are **20%**, $\frac{4}{20}$
and **0.2** *(1 mark)*

Q6 $30\% = \frac{30}{100} = \frac{3}{10}$
$1600 \div 10 = 160$
$160 \times 3 = 480$
Jim gives £480 to charity.
$1500 \div 5 = 300$
$300 \times 2 = 600$
Jack gives £600 to charity.
Jack gives more money.
*(2 marks for correct
answer, otherwise 1 mark
for working out either
£480 or £600.)*

Q7 $\frac{5}{8} = 5 \div 8$
$= (5000 \div 8) \div 1000$
$\quad\quad 0\ 6\ 2\ 5$
$8\,\overline{)5\,5^50^20\,0}$
$= 625 \div 1000 = \mathbf{0.625}$
(1 mark)

Section Four — Ratio and Proportion

Pages 30-31 — Relative Sizes

Q1 $35 \times 5 = 175p = \mathbf{£1.75}$
(1 mark)

Q2 $£1.80 = 180p$
$180 \div 4 = \mathbf{45p}$ *(1 mark)*

Q3 $6 \times 7 = \mathbf{£42}$ *(1 mark)*

Q4 $32 \div 8 = 4$
$4 \times 5 = \mathbf{20\ pupils}$ *(1 mark)*

Q5 The ratio is £30 to 4
membership points
(£30:4 membership
points). £180 is 6 lots
of £30. So $6 \times 4 =$
24 points. *(1 mark)*

Q6 $450 \div 150 = 3$
$3 \times 250 = \mathbf{750\ g}$
chocolate *(1 mark)*
150:75 or **2:1**
(1 mark)

Q7 $48 \div 6 = 8$
So there are 8 teams.
There are 2 adults in each
team. So there are 8×2
$= \mathbf{16\ adults}$ *(1 mark)*

Pages 32-33 — Scale Factors

Q1
(1 mark)

Q2 Scale factor = **3** *(1 mark)*

Q3
(1 mark)

Q4 $60 \div 12 = \mathbf{5\ cm}$ *(1 mark)*

Q5
(1 mark)
(1 mark)
Base of A = 2
Base of C = 12
Scale factor = $12 \div 2 = \mathbf{6}$
(1 mark)

Pages 34-35 — Percentages of Amounts

Q1 10% of 200 = 200 ÷ 10
$= \mathbf{20}$ *(1 mark)*
10% of 750 = 750 ÷ 10
$= 75$
30% of 750 = 3 × 75
$= \mathbf{225}$ *(1 mark)*
10% of 600 = 600 ÷ 10
$= 60$
40% of 600 = 4 × 60
$= \mathbf{240}$ *(1 mark)*
10% of 850 = 850 ÷ 10
$= 85$
60% of 850 = 6 × 85
$= \mathbf{510}$ *(1 mark)*

Q2 10% of 300 = 300 ÷ 10
$= 30$
5% of 300 = 30 ÷ 2 = 15
15% of 300 = 30 + 15
$= \mathbf{45}$ *(1 mark)*
10% of 360 = 360 ÷ 10
$= 36$
20% of 360 = 2 × 36
$= 72$
5% of 360 = 36 ÷ 2 = 18
25% of 360 = 72 + 18
$= \mathbf{90}$ *(1 mark)*
50% of 440 = 440 ÷ 2
$= 220$
5% of 440 = 220 ÷ 10
$= 22$
55% of 440 = 220 + 22
$= \mathbf{242}$ *(1 mark)*
10% of 120 = 120 ÷ 10
$= 12$
5% of 120 = 12 ÷ 2 = 6
95% of 120 = 120 − 6
$= \mathbf{114}$ *(1 mark)*

Q3 £3.80 = 380p
10% of 380 = 380 ÷ 10
$= 38$
20% of 380 = 38 × 2
$= 76$
5% of 380 = 38 ÷ 2 = 19
76 + 19 = 95p
380 − 95 = 285p = **£2.85**
(1 mark)

Q4 10% of 160 = 160 ÷ 10
$= 16$
20% of 160 = 16 × 2
$= 32$
5% of 160 = 16 ÷ 2 = 8
32 + 8 = 40

Answers

10% of 140 = 140 ÷ 10
= 14
40% of 140 = 14 × 4
= 56
So **25% of £160** is smaller. *(1 mark)*

Q5   10% of 360° = 360° ÷ 10
= 36°
60% of 360° = 36° × 6
= 216°
5% of 360° = 36° ÷ 2
= 18°
216° + 18° = **234°**
(1 mark)

Q6   10% of 120 = 120 ÷ 10
= 12
40% of 120 = 4 × 12
= 48
5% of 120 = 12 ÷ 2 = 6
45% = 48 + 6 = 54
120 − 54 = 66
66 people prefer biscuits at lunch time. *(1 mark)*

Q7   10% of 12 = 12 ÷ 10
= 1.2
20% of 12 = 2 × 1.2
= 2.4
12 − 2.4 = 9.6
So jumpers cost £9.60.
10% of 8 = 8 ÷ 10 = 0.8
5% of 8 = 0.8 ÷ 2 = 0.4
15% of 8 = 0.4 + 0.8
= 1.2
8 − 1.2 = 6.8
So t-shirts cost £6.80.
£9.60 + £9.60 + £6.80
= £26
Dan spends **£26**. *(1 mark)*
£12 + £12 + £8 = £32
£32 − £26 = £6
Dan saves **£6** off the original price. *(1 mark)*

Pages 36-37 — Comparing Using Percentages

Q1 $\frac{160}{400} = \frac{40}{100} = \mathbf{40\%}$
(1 mark)

Q2   200 − 40 = 160
$\frac{160}{200} = \frac{80}{100} = \mathbf{80\%}$
(1 mark)

Q3   1500 − 1050 = 450
$\frac{450}{1500} = \frac{30}{100} = \mathbf{30\%}$
(1 mark)

Q4   5 + 8 + 7 = 20
$\frac{8}{20} = \frac{40}{100} = \mathbf{40\%}$
(1 mark)

Q5   Kayleigh's clothes had a discount of:
$\frac{5}{50} = \frac{10}{100} = 10\%$
Rachael's clothes had a discount of:
$\frac{3}{20} = \frac{15}{100} = 15\%$
So **Rachael's** clothes had the biggest percentage discount. *(1 mark)*

Q6   500 − 250 = 250
$\frac{250}{500} = \frac{50}{100} = 50\%$
400 − 180 = 220
$\frac{220}{400} = \frac{55}{100} = 55\%$
So **Johnny** has the highest percentage of his drink left. *(1 mark)*

Q7   35 + 15 = 50
$\frac{15}{50} = \frac{30}{100} = \mathbf{30\%}$
(1 mark)
10% of 15 = 15 ÷ 10
= 1.5
20% of 15 = 2 × 1.5 = 3
10% of 35 = 35 ÷ 10
= 3.5
40% of 35 = 4 × 3.5 = 14
50 − 3 − 14 = 33
$\frac{33}{50} = \frac{66}{100} = 66\%$
66% of all the players are uninjured. *(1 mark)*

Pages 38-39 — Unequal Sharing

Q1   12 × 4 = **48 chickens**
(1 mark)
15 ÷ 3 = **5 cows**
(1 mark)

Q2   6 potatoes is 3 times as many as 2.
So James will have
3 × 3 = **9 carrots**
(1 mark)

4 potatoes is twice as many as 2.
So Mila will have
2 × 7 = **14 green beans**
(1 mark)

Q3   18 ÷ 6 = 3
3 × 4 = **12 peaches**
(1 mark)
18 ÷ 3 = 6
6 × 5 = **30 strawberries**
(1 mark)

Q4   In the reptile house the ratio of snakes to lizards is 3:2. There are 3 + 2 = 5 shares. 100 ÷ 5 = 20, so 2 × 20 = **40 lizards**
(1 mark)

Q5   There are 2 + 5 = 7 shares. 14 ÷ 7 = 2.
So Georgetown score
2 × 2 = **4 goals**. *(1 mark)*
Hatville score 5 × 2
= **10 goals** *(1 mark)*

Q6   They are sharing cheese sandwiches in the ratio 3:1, so there are 4 shares.
8 ÷ 4 = 2
3 × 2 = 6, so Ben gets 6 cheese sandwiches.
They are sharing ham sandwiches in the ratio 1:2, so there are 3 shares.
9 ÷ 3 = 3
So Ben gets 3 ham sandwiches.
6 + 3 = 9, so Ben gets **9 sandwiches** in total.
(1 mark)

Section Five — Algebra

Pages 40-41 — Sequences

Q1   13 − 1 = 12
25 − 13 = 12
So the rule is **add 12**.
(1 mark)

Q2   6, 11, **16**, **21**, **26**
(1 mark)

Q3   36, 32, **28**, **24**, **20**
(1 mark)

Q4   The rule is take 7.
29, 22, 15, **8**, **1**
(1 mark)

Answers

Q5 The rule is add 6.
-12, -6, **0**, 6, 12, **18**
(1 mark)

Q6 The rule is add 11.
To find the first two terms,
count back:
87 – 11 = **76**
76 – 11 = **65**
(1 mark)

Q7 37 – 30 = -7
23 – 30 = -7
So the rule is **take 7**.
(1 mark)
The 5th term is 9. To find
the 8th term take 7 three
more times.
9 – 7 – 7– 7= **-12**
(1 mark)

Q8 The difference between 7
and -5 is 12. There are 3
steps between 7 and -5.
12 ÷ 3 = 4, so:
7 – 4 = **3**
3 – 4 = **-1** *(1 mark)*
The difference between
53 and 9 is 44. There are
4 steps between 53 and 9.
44 ÷ 4 = 11, so:
53 – 11 = **42**
42 – 11 = **31**
31 – 11 = **20**
(1 mark)

Pages 42-43 — Missing Number Problems

Q1 To find John's age, you
add 12 to Sam's age, then
divide by 3.

$(3) \rightarrow +12 \rightarrow \div 3 \rightarrow (j)$

Sam is 3, so John is **5**
years old. *(1 mark)*

Q2 54 – 9 = 45
3☆ = 45
☆ = 45 ÷ 3 = **15**
So Amir was thinking of
the number **15**. *(1 mark)*

Q3 △ = 24 ÷ 4 = **6** *(1 mark)*
□ = 13 – 7 = **6** *(1 mark)*
○ = 9 + 5 = **14** *(1 mark)*

Q4 p = 12, so 12 = 3j
12 ÷ 3 = j
12 ÷ 3 = 4
j = 4, so Jen has **4 badges**.
(1 mark)

Q5 Rob has 2 × the number
of muffins Matt has, so
2m = r. *(1 mark)*

Q6 The caterpillar eats
4 × the number of leaves
the slug eats, so **c = 4s**.
(1 mark)

Q7 s = (2 + 1) × 6
s = 3 × 6 = 18
So there are **18**
strawberries in the
smoothie. *(1 mark)*

Pages 44-45 — Two Missing Numbers

Q1 Some possible pairs are:
A = 1   B = 12
A = 2   B = 6
A = 3   B = 4
*(2 marks for 3 correct
pairs, otherwise 1 mark
for 2 correct pairs.)*

Q2 E.g.
C = 10   D = 0
C = 6   D = 1
C = 2   D = 2
*(2 marks for all three pairs,
otherwise 1 mark for
2 correct pairs.)*

Q3 Some possible pairs are:
M = 1   N = 12
M = 2   N = 6
M = 3   N = 4
M = 4   N = 3
*(2 marks for 3 correct
pairs, otherwise 1 mark
for 2 correct pairs.)*

Q4 i = 6   s = 0
i = 4   s = 1
i = 2   s = 2
i = 0   s = 3
*(2 marks for all pairs
correct, otherwise 1 mark
for 2 or 3 pairs correct.)*

Q5 I + J + I + K + J = 36,
which is the same as
2I + 2J + K = 36.
I = 10, so
20 + 2J + K = 36
2J + K = 16
Possible pairs are:
J = 0   K = 16
J = 1   K = 14
J = 2   K = 12
J = 4   K = 8
J = 5   K = 6
J = 6   K = 4
J = 7   K = 2
J = 8   K = 0
*(2 marks for 3 correct
pairs, otherwise 1 mark
for 2 correct pairs.)*

Pages 46-47 — Formulas

Q1 Number of cookies
= 8 × 4 = **32 cookies**
(1 mark)

Q2 Area = 7 × 4 = **28 cm²**
(1 mark)

Q3 Amount of flour
= (11 × 12) + 10 = **142 g**
(1 mark)

Q4 Time = $\dfrac{(160 \times 4) + 80}{4}$
= 720 ÷ 4 = **180 minutes**
(1 mark)

Q5 **Points = 5 × number of
goals** *(1 mark)*

Q6 **Cost = 16 × number of
apples** *(1 mark)*
Cost = 16 × 3 = **48p**
(1 mark)

Q7 **Cost = 5 + 2 × number of
hoops** *(1 mark)*
Cost = 5 + (2 × 8) =
5 + 16 = **21p** *(1 mark)*

Section Six — Measurement
Pages 48-49 — Units

Q1 1 litre = 1000 ml
10.8 × 1000 = **10 800 ml**
(1 mark)

Q2 1 kg = 1000 g
258 ÷ 1000 = **0.258 kg**
(1 mark)

Answers

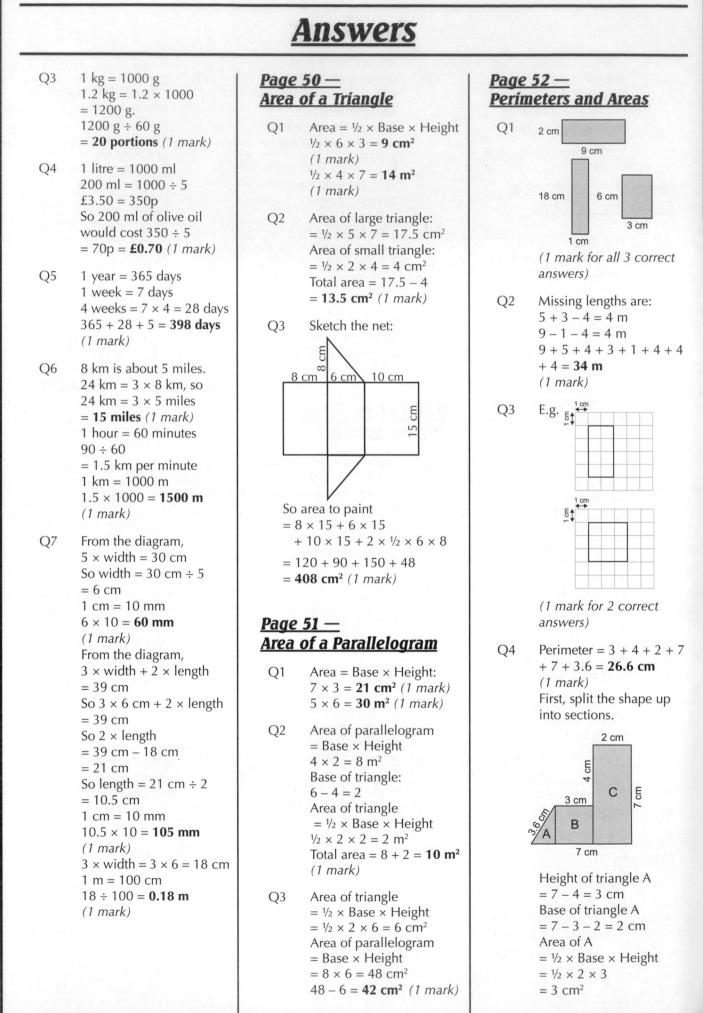

Q3 1 kg = 1000 g
1.2 kg = 1.2 × 1000
= 1200 g.
1200 g ÷ 60 g
= **20 portions** *(1 mark)*

Q4 1 litre = 1000 ml
200 ml = 1000 ÷ 5
£3.50 = 350p
So 200 ml of olive oil
would cost 350 ÷ 5
= 70p = **£0.70** *(1 mark)*

Q5 1 year = 365 days
1 week = 7 days
4 weeks = 7 × 4 = 28 days
365 + 28 + 5 = **398 days**
(1 mark)

Q6 8 km is about 5 miles.
24 km = 3 × 8 km, so
24 km = 3 × 5 miles
= **15 miles** *(1 mark)*
1 hour = 60 minutes
90 ÷ 60
= 1.5 km per minute
1 km = 1000 m
1.5 × 1000 = **1500 m**
(1 mark)

Q7 From the diagram,
5 × width = 30 cm
So width = 30 cm ÷ 5
= 6 cm
1 cm = 10 mm
6 × 10 = **60 mm**
(1 mark)
From the diagram,
3 × width + 2 × length
= 39 cm
So 3 × 6 cm + 2 × length
= 39 cm
So 2 × length
= 39 cm – 18 cm
= 21 cm
So length = 21 cm ÷ 2
= 10.5 cm
1 cm = 10 mm
10.5 × 10 = **105 mm**
(1 mark)
3 × width = 3 × 6 = 18 cm
1 m = 100 cm
18 ÷ 100 = **0.18 m**
(1 mark)

Page 50 —
Area of a Triangle

Q1 Area = ½ × Base × Height
½ × 6 × 3 = **9 cm²**
(1 mark)
½ × 4 × 7 = **14 m²**
(1 mark)

Q2 Area of large triangle:
= ½ × 5 × 7 = 17.5 cm²
Area of small triangle:
= ½ × 2 × 4 = 4 cm²
Total area = 17.5 – 4
= **13.5 cm²** *(1 mark)*

Q3 Sketch the net:

So area to paint
= 8 × 15 + 6 × 15
  + 10 × 15 + 2 × ½ × 6 × 8
= 120 + 90 + 150 + 48
= **408 cm²** *(1 mark)*

Page 51 —
Area of a Parallelogram

Q1 Area = Base × Height:
7 × 3 = **21 cm²** *(1 mark)*
5 × 6 = **30 m²** *(1 mark)*

Q2 Area of parallelogram
= Base × Height
4 × 2 = 8 m²
Base of triangle:
6 – 4 = 2
Area of triangle
 = ½ × Base × Height
½ × 2 × 2 = 2 m²
Total area = 8 + 2 = **10 m²**
(1 mark)

Q3 Area of triangle
= ½ × Base × Height
= ½ × 2 × 6 = 6 cm²
Area of parallelogram
= Base × Height
= 8 × 6 = 48 cm²
48 – 6 = **42 cm²** *(1 mark)*

Page 52 —
Perimeters and Areas

Q1 2 cm
9 cm
18 cm   6 cm
1 cm   3 cm
*(1 mark for all 3 correct
answers)*

Q2 Missing lengths are:
5 + 3 – 4 = 4 m
9 – 1 – 4 = 4 m
9 + 5 + 4 + 3 + 1 + 4 + 4
+ 4 = **34 m**
(1 mark)

Q3 E.g.

*(1 mark for 2 correct
answers)*

Q4 Perimeter = 3 + 4 + 2 + 7
+ 7 + 3.6 = **26.6 cm**
(1 mark)
First, split the shape up
into sections.

Height of triangle A
= 7 – 4 = 3 cm
Base of triangle A
= 7 – 3 – 2 = 2 cm
Area of A
= ½ × Base × Height
= ½ × 2 × 3
= 3 cm²

Answers

Area of B = 3 × 3 = 9 cm²
Area of C = 2 × 7
= 14 cm²
3 + 9 + 14 = **26 cm²**
(1 mark)

Page 53 — Volumes of Cubes and Cuboids

Q1 Volume = Length × Width × Height
4 × 2 × 4 = **32 m³**
(1 mark)

Q2 Volume = Length × Width × Height
3 × 3 × 3 = **27 km³**
(1 mark)

Q3 Split the shape into sections down the dotted line, then work out the volume of each section and add them together.

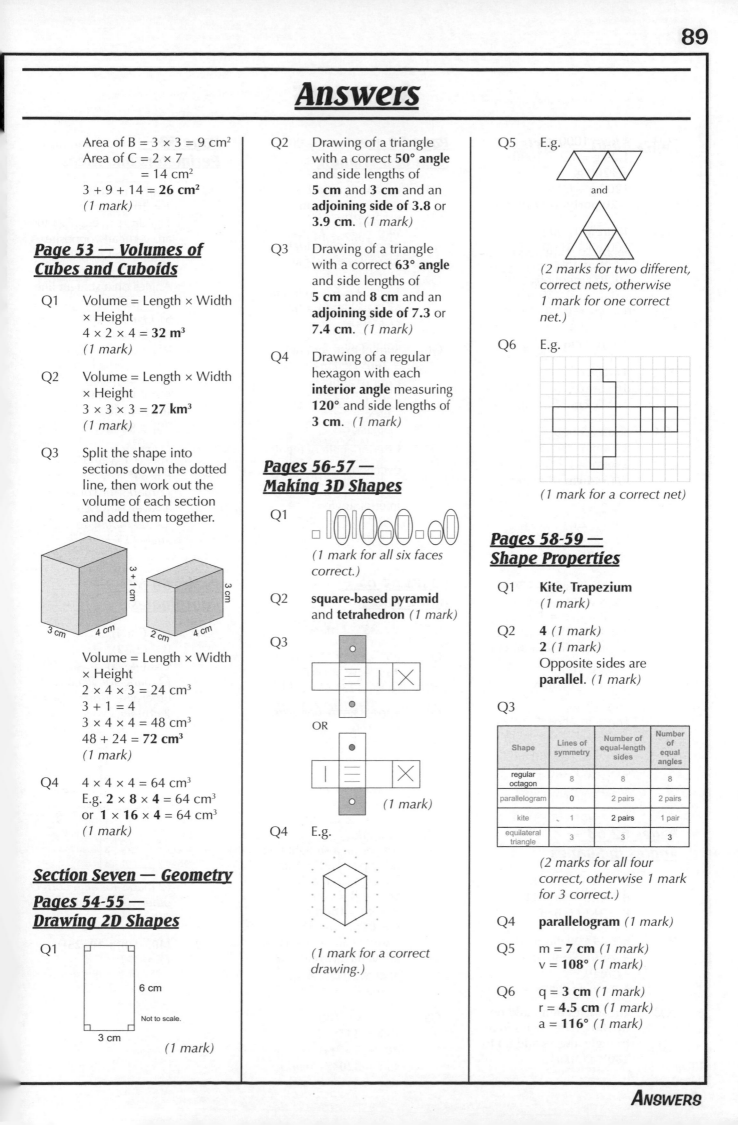

Volume = Length × Width × Height
2 × 4 × 3 = 24 cm³
3 + 1 = 4
3 × 4 × 4 = 48 cm³
48 + 24 = **72 cm³**
(1 mark)

Q4 4 × 4 × 4 = 64 cm³
E.g. **2 × 8 × 4** = 64 cm³
or **1 × 16 × 4** = 64 cm³
(1 mark)

Section Seven — Geometry

Pages 54-55 — Drawing 2D Shapes

Q1

6 cm

Not to scale.

3 cm

(1 mark)

Q2 Drawing of a triangle with a correct **50° angle** and side lengths of **5 cm** and **3 cm** and an **adjoining side of 3.8** or **3.9 cm**. *(1 mark)*

Q3 Drawing of a triangle with a correct **63° angle** and side lengths of **5 cm** and **8 cm** and an **adjoining side of 7.3** or **7.4 cm**. *(1 mark)*

Q4 Drawing of a regular hexagon with each **interior angle** measuring **120°** and side lengths of **3 cm**. *(1 mark)*

Pages 56-57 — Making 3D Shapes

Q1

(1 mark for all six faces correct.)

Q2 **square-based pyramid** and **tetrahedron** *(1 mark)*

Q3

OR

(1 mark)

Q4 E.g.

(1 mark for a correct drawing.)

Q5 E.g.

and

(2 marks for two different, correct nets, otherwise 1 mark for one correct net.)

Q6 E.g.

(1 mark for a correct net)

Pages 58-59 — Shape Properties

Q1 **Kite, Trapezium**
(1 mark)

Q2 **4** *(1 mark)*
2 *(1 mark)*
Opposite sides are **parallel**. *(1 mark)*

Q3

Shape	Lines of symmetry	Number of equal-length sides	Number of equal angles
regular octagon	8	8	8
parallelogram	0	2 pairs	2 pairs
kite	1	**2 pairs**	1 pair
equilateral triangle	3	3	3

(2 marks for all four correct, otherwise 1 mark for 3 correct.)

Q4 **parallelogram** *(1 mark)*

Q5 m = **7 cm** *(1 mark)*
v = **108°** *(1 mark)*

Q6 q = **3 cm** *(1 mark)*
r = **4.5 cm** *(1 mark)*
a = **116°** *(1 mark)*

Answers

Pages 60-61 — Circles

Q1

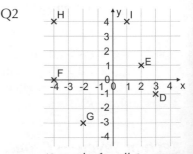

(1 mark for drawing an arrow pointing to anywhere on the outside edge of the circle.)

Q2 d = 2 × r
d = 2 × 50
d = **100 cm** *(1 mark)*

Q3 d = 2 × r
d = 2 × 6
d = **12 cm** *(1 mark)*

Q4 d = 2 × r
8 = 2 × r
8 = 2 × 4
so r = **4 cm** *(1 mark)*

Q5 d = 2 × r
70 = 2 × r
70 = 2 × 35
so r = **35 cm** *(1 mark)*

Q6 Radius of Janet's circle
= 3 × 5 cm = 15 cm.
d = 2 × r. d = 2 × 15
d = 30 so the diameter of Janet's circle = **30 cm**.
(1 mark)

Q7 d = 2 × r
160 = 2 × r
160 = 2 × 80
so r = 80 cm
40 + x + 10 = 80 cm
so x = 80 – 40 – 10
x = **30 cm** *(1 mark)*

Pages 62-63 — Angles in Shapes

Q1 B + 54 + 90 = 180
B = 180 – 90 – 54
B = **36°** *(1 mark)*

Q2 x + 247° + 42° + 51°
= 360°
x + 340° = 360°
x = **20°** *(1 mark)*

Q3 **The angles don't add up to 180°. The angles in a triangle always add up to 180°.** *(1 mark)*

Q4 t + 102° + 90° + 90°
= 360°
t + 282° = 360°
t = **78°** *(1 mark)*

Q5 e + f + 46 = 180
so e + f = 180 – 46 = 134
It's an isosceles triangle so angles e and f are equal.
134 ÷ 2 = 67, so **e = 67°** *(1 mark)* and **f = 67°** *(1 mark)*.

Q6 Sum of exterior angles
= **360°** *(1 mark)*
Exterior angle =
$\frac{360°}{n} = \frac{360°}{8} = $ **45°**
(1 mark)

Q7 Exterior angle of regular decagon = $\frac{360°}{10} = $ **36°**
(1 mark)
Interior angle =
180° – 36° = **144°**
(1 mark)

Pages 64-65 — Angle Rules

Q1 T = **33°** *(1 mark)*

Q2 65° + 90° + W = 180°
155° + W = 180°
so W = **25°** *(1 mark)*

Q3 100° + 80° + 90° + 76° +
G = 360°
346° + G = 360°
so G = **14°** *(1 mark)*

Q4 A and C are equal as they are vertically opposite angles, so C = **99°**
(1 mark).
Angles on a straight line add up to 180°. A and B are on a straight line.
So A + B = 180°
A + 99 = 180°
B = **81°** *(1 mark)*
B and D are equal as they are vertically opposite angles, so D = **81°**
(1 mark).

Q5 65° + X = 180°
so X = **115°** *(1 mark)*
40° + Y = 360°
so Y = **320°** *(1 mark)*

Q6 It's an isosceles triangle so angle S = 75°.
75° + 75° + T = 180°
150° + T = 180°
T = 30°
T and Q are equal as they are vertically opposite angles, so Q = **30°**
(1 mark).
Angles on a straight line add up to 180°.
So Q + R = 180°
R + 30 = 180°
R = **150°** *(1 mark)*

Q7 20° + 20° + Q = 180°
40° + Q = 180°
so Q = 140°
70° + 90° + 140° + P
= 360°
300° + P = 360°
P = **60°**
(2 marks for correct answer, otherwise 1 mark for attempting to find angle Q.)

Pages 66-67 — Coordinates

Q1 A = **(-3, 4)**
B = **(2, -2)**
C = **(-4, -3)**
(2 marks for all correct, otherwise 1 mark for 2 correct.)

Q2

(2 marks for all 6 correct, otherwise 1 mark for 4 or 5 correct.)

Q3 **(40, -10), (-10, 25)**
(1 mark)

Answers

Q4 The triangles are both 4 units high and 4 units wide. Point B has an x-coordinate of 4 + 4 = 8 and a y-coordinate of 4 + 4 = 8. So point B has coordinates **(8, 8)** *(1 mark)*.
Point C is on the same horizontal line as (4, 4) so its y-coordinate is 4. It is on the same vertical line as (8, 8), so its x-coordinate is 8. So point C has coordinates **(8, 4)** *(1 mark)*.

Q5 Point D must have the same x-coordinate as the opposite triangle, so its x-coordinate is 7. The height of the opposite triangle is 10 – 3 = 7. As the two triangles are the same height point D must have a y-coordinate of 3 – 7 = -4. So point D has coordinates **(7, -4)** *(1 mark)*.

Q6 Point Z is on the same horizontal line as (21, 18), so its y-coordinate is 18. As it's a parallelogram the top side is the same length as the bottom side. The length of the bottom side is 15 – 6 = 9. So the x-coordinate of the top side is 21 – 9 = 12. Point Z has coordinates **(12, 18)** *(1 mark)*.

Page 68 — Reflection

Q1

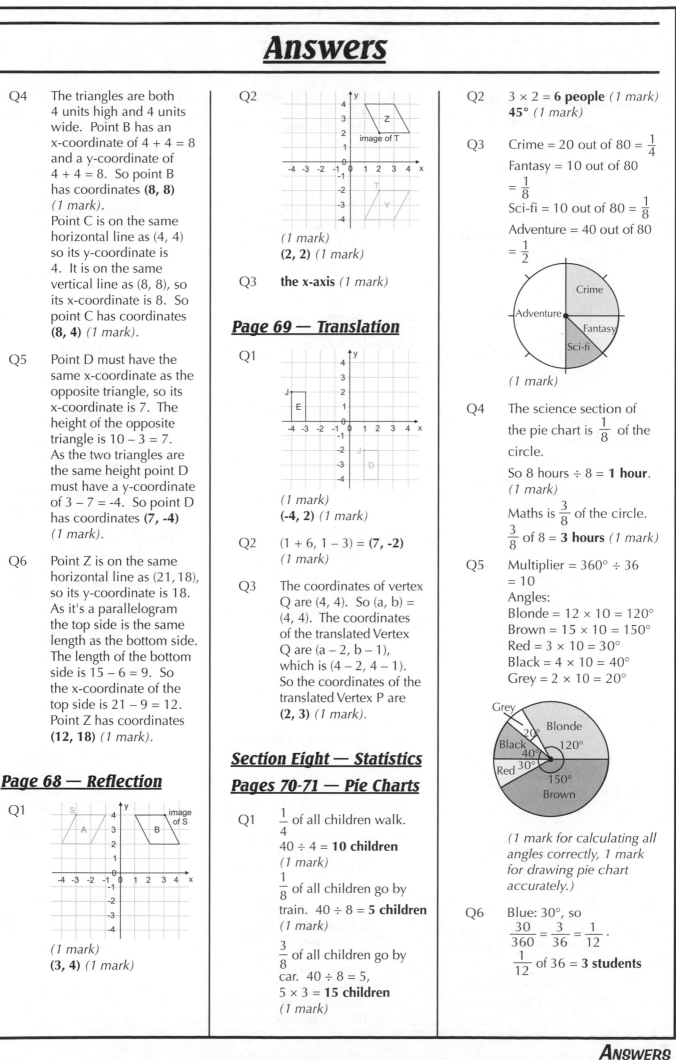

(1 mark)
(3, 4) *(1 mark)*

Q2

(1 mark)
(2, 2) *(1 mark)*

Q3 **the x-axis** *(1 mark)*

Page 69 — Translation

Q1

(1 mark)
(-4, 2) *(1 mark)*

Q2 (1 + 6, 1 – 3) = **(7, -2)** *(1 mark)*

Q3 The coordinates of vertex Q are (4, 4). So (a, b) = (4, 4). The coordinates of the translated Vertex Q are (a – 2, b – 1), which is (4 – 2, 4 – 1). So the coordinates of the translated Vertex P are **(2, 3)** *(1 mark)*.

Section Eight — Statistics

Pages 70-71 — Pie Charts

Q1 $\frac{1}{4}$ of all children walk. 40 ÷ 4 = **10 children** *(1 mark)*
$\frac{1}{8}$ of all children go by train. 40 ÷ 8 = **5 children** *(1 mark)*
$\frac{3}{8}$ of all children go by car. 40 ÷ 8 = 5, 5 × 3 = **15 children** *(1 mark)*

Q2 3 × 2 = **6 people** *(1 mark)*
45° *(1 mark)*

Q3 Crime = 20 out of 80 = $\frac{1}{4}$
Fantasy = 10 out of 80 = $\frac{1}{8}$
Sci-fi = 10 out of 80 = $\frac{1}{8}$
Adventure = 40 out of 80 = $\frac{1}{2}$

(1 mark)

Q4 The science section of the pie chart is $\frac{1}{8}$ of the circle.
So 8 hours ÷ 8 = **1 hour**. *(1 mark)*
Maths is $\frac{3}{8}$ of the circle.
$\frac{3}{8}$ of 8 = **3 hours** *(1 mark)*

Q5 Multiplier = 360° ÷ 36 = 10
Angles:
Blonde = 12 × 10 = 120°
Brown = 15 × 10 = 150°
Red = 3 × 10 = 30°
Black = 4 × 10 = 40°
Grey = 2 × 10 = 20°

(1 mark for calculating all angles correctly, 1 mark for drawing pie chart accurately.)

Q6 Blue: 30°, so $\frac{30}{360} = \frac{3}{36} = \frac{1}{12}$.
$\frac{1}{12}$ of 36 = **3 students**

Answers

Red: 80°, so
$$\frac{80}{360} = \frac{8}{36} = \frac{2}{9}$$
$\frac{2}{9}$ of 36 = 36 ÷ 9 = 4,
4 × 2 = **8 students**
Purple: 110°, so
$$\frac{110}{360} = \frac{11}{36}.$$
$\frac{11}{36}$ of 36 = **11 students**
Beige: 140°, so
$$\frac{140}{360} = \frac{14}{36}.$$
$\frac{14}{36}$ of 36 = **14 students**
(2 marks for all correct, otherwise 1 mark for 2 or 3 correct.)

Pages 72-73 — Line Graphs

Q1   20 − 5 = **15** *(1 mark)*
Between **1:30 pm** and **2:00 pm**. *(1 mark)*

Q2   **5.5 lbs** — allow 5.4-5.6 lbs *(1 mark)*

Q3
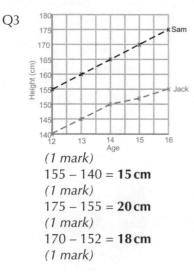
(1 mark)
155 − 140 = **15 cm** *(1 mark)*
175 − 155 = **20 cm** *(1 mark)*
170 − 152 = **18 cm** *(1 mark)*

Pages 74-75 — The Mean

Q1   7 + 8 + 3 + 6 + 11 + 4 + 10 = 49
49 ÷ 7 = **7** *(1 mark)*

Q2   6 + 9 + 13 + 10 + 7 = 45
45 ÷ 5 = **9 °C** *(1 mark)*

Q3   Paolo's mean was
7 + 6 + 8 + 5 + 4 = 30
30 ÷ 5 = **6 falls** *(1 mark)*

Q4   40 + 55 + 15 + 45 + 70 + 45 + 10 = 280.
280 ÷ 7 = **40 cars** *(1 mark)*

Q5   (100 × 3) + (20 × 4) + (300 × 1) + (40 × 1) + (25 × 2)
= 300 + 80 + 300 + 40 + 50 = **770p** *(1 mark)*
3 + 4 + 1 + 1 + 2 = **11** *(1 mark)*
770 ÷ 11 = **70p** *(1 mark)*

Pages 76-79 — Year Six Objectives Test

Q1 $\frac{1}{3} = \frac{7}{21}$ and $\frac{2}{7} = \frac{6}{21}$
so $\frac{1}{3}$ **is the largest.**
(1 mark for correct answer and explanation.)

Q2   -51 − 7 = **-44**
-44 − 7 = **-37** *(1 mark)*

Q3 $\frac{5}{3} \times \frac{2}{6} = \frac{5 \times 2}{3 \times 6}$
$= \frac{10}{18} = \frac{5}{9}$ *(1 mark)*

Q4   36 ÷ 12 = 3
3 × 150 = **450 g** *(1 mark)*

Q5   (7 + 2) × 3 − 4 = 23 *(1 mark)*

Q6   The rectangle must be 9 squares wide and 6 squares high. *(1 mark)*

Q7   12 × 4 × 6 = **288 cm³** *(1 mark)*

Q8   10% = 60 ÷ 10 = 6
5% = 6 ÷ 2 = 3
15% = 6 + 3 = **9** *(1 mark)*

Q9   Area = Base × Height
54 = 9 × Height
Height = 54 ÷ 9 = **6 cm** *(1 mark)*

Q10 The x-coordinate of B is the same as the x-coordinate of C, and the y-coordinate of B is the same as the y-coordinate of A, so the coordinates of B are **(15, 7)**. *(1 mark)*

Q11
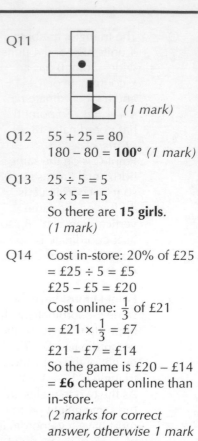
(1 mark)

Q12 55 + 25 = 80
180 − 80 = **100°** *(1 mark)*

Q13 25 ÷ 5 = 5
3 × 5 = 15
So there are **15 girls**. *(1 mark)*

Q14 Cost in-store: 20% of £25 = £25 ÷ 5 = £5
£25 − £5 = £20
Cost online: $\frac{1}{3}$ of £21 = £21 × $\frac{1}{3}$ = £7
£21 − £7 = £14
So the game is £20 − £14 = **£6** cheaper online than in-store.
(2 marks for correct answer, otherwise 1 mark for suitable working.)

Q15

Flavour	Angle in pie chart
Strawberry	120°
Vanilla	**80°**
Mint	**60°**
Chocolate	**100°**

(1 mark for completing table correctly and 1 mark for correctly-drawn pie chart. Sections may be in any order but angles must be correct to within 1°.)

Q16 $12\overline{)7860}$ = 655 *(1 mark)*

Q17 2M = 25 − 7 = 18
M = 18 ÷ 2 = **9** *(1 mark)*